ATLAS OF THE
ENVIRONMENT

RSVP

RAINTREE
STECK-VAUGHN
P U B L I S H E R S
Austin, Texas

111513

Editor: Roger Coote
Designer: Ross George
Cover designer: Suzanne Beck
Cartography: Swanston Graphics, Ltd.

Typeset by Tom Fenton Studio, Neptune, NJ
Printed by Rotolito Lombarda , S.p.A., Milan
Bound by Lake Book, Melrose Park, IL

1 2 3 4 5 6 7 8 9 0 LB 98 97 96 95 94 93

Library of Congress Cataloging-in-Publication Data
Steck-Vaughn Company.
    Atlas of the environment / editor, Roger Coote.
       p.   cm.
    Includes bibliographical references (p.   ) and index.
    Summary: Maps, photographs, and text examine the planet's endangered environment and possible future.
    ISBN 0-8114-7250-7
    1. Human ecology — Juvenile literature.   2. Conservation of natural resources — Juvenile literature.   3. Pollution — Juvenile literature.   4. Environmental protection — Juvenile literature.
    [1. Environmental protection.   2. Man — Influence on nature.   3. Human ecology.   4. Ecology.]   I. Coote, Roger.
GF48.A85   1993   92-8196
363.7 — dc20   CIP AC

Picture Acknowledgments

The publishers would like to thank the following for allowing their pictures to be reproduced in this book:
Bruce Coleman Ltd 8 (John Cancalosi), 11 (Leonard Lee Rue III), 21 (Alain Compost), 25 (Michael Fogden), 27 bottom (N.G. Blake), 30-31 (Hans Reinhard), 34 (Gerald Cubitt), 34-35 (Nicholas Devore), 39 bottom (Udo Hirsch), 41 (Henneghien), 45 (Peter Davey), 52-53 (Hans-Peter Merten), 60-61 (Robert P. Carr), 75 (N.G. Blake), 81 (C. James), 86 (Chris James), 87 bottom (J. Cancalosi); Frank Lane 10 (C. Carvalho), 27 top (Derek Hall), 47 bottom (Jean Hosking); Greenpeace 67 (Edwards), 69 (Walker), 90 (Perez); Hutchison Library 28-29, 31, 36, 62, 72-73 (Michael Macintyre), 76; ICCE front cover lower middle (John Parrott), 83 top (Mark Boulton), 84 (Rob Cousins); ICI Fibres 50; Miriam Moss 83 bottom; Courtesy NASA 4; Oxford Scientific Films front cover bottom (Frank Huber), 9 (Michael Fogden), 13 and cover upper middle (Doug Allan), 29 (Richard Kolar/Earth Scenes), 36-37 (Tim Shepherd), 50-51 (John McCammon), 59 top (Lena Beyer), 68 (Kim Westerskov), 89 (Stan Osolinski); Panos Pictures 12 top (Alain Le Garsmeur), 16-17 (Paul Harrison), 18-19 (Ron Giling), 19 (Ron Giling), 20 (Ron Giling), 26 (Michael Harvey), 39 top (Ron Giling), 43 (Ron Giling), 44-45 (Bruce Paton), 63 and cover top (Jeremy Hartley); Papilio 73; Planet Earth Pictures 8-9 (J. Scott), 12 bottom (Peter David), 24 (Richard Beales), 47 top (John Lythgoe), 53 (Brian Coope), 62-63 (J. Bracegirdle), 91 (Nigel Merrett); Topham Picture Source 35 (Hans Silvester/Rapho), 54 (Associated Press), 70 (Associated Press), 70-71 (Associated Press) 76-77 (Associated Press), 77 (Associated Press), 78-79 (Associated Press), 80 (Associated Press); Wayland Picture Library 55, 59 bottom, 66-67; Zefa 15 (Justitz), 57 (Bob Croxford), 79 (Davies), 87 top (Griffith). All maps and diagrams are by Swanston Graphics Ltd. Front cover artwork is by Suzanne Beck.

LIST OF CONTRIBUTORS

INTRODUCTION — **John Howson** is education officer for the environmental organization Friends of the Earth.

THE NATURAL WORLD — **Andrew Kelley** is an environmentalist and a writer and editor of books for children. He lives and works in Victoria, Australia.

THE HUMAN WORLD — **Stephen Sterling** is a researcher, writer, and lecturer on environmental matters and a consultant in environmental education.

FALLING FORESTS — **Liz Chidley,** formerly of the World Wide Fund for Nature, now works as a freelance researcher and writer.

FOOD AND FARMING —**Hannah Pearce** trained as an environmentalist and later worked for Friends of the Earth. She is now a freelance journalist.

DESERTIFICATION — **Dr. Ewan McLeish** is the director of the Council for Environmental Education in England. He has written widely on environmental issues, and is the author of *The Spread of Deserts* in Steck-Vaughn's "Conserving Our World" series.

ENERGY CRISIS — **Damian Randle,** formerly education officer at the Center for Alternative Technology in Machnylleth, Wales, is now the editor of *Green Teacher* magazine. He is also a freelance writer and researcher.

AIR POLLUTION — **John Baines** is an ex-teacher and former director of the Council for Environmental Education. He is a well-known freelance writer and researcher and is the author of *Protecting the Oceans* and *Acid Rain* in Steck-Vaughn's "Conserving Our World" series.

POLLUTED WATERS — **Dr. René Heijnis,** who lives in Zaandam, the Netherlands, is a specialist in environmental biology and ecology. He has been a member of the Examination Group of the Dutch Department of Education and is the author of a number of educational books and materials.

CLIMATE UNDER THREAT — **Robert Harris** worked in Africa for several years and has written for the United Nations Council of Refugees in Nairobi and for the Canadian International Development Agency. He now lives in Canada where he is a library consultant and works on school environmental projects for an educational publisher.

CONSERVING OUR WORLD — **Barbara James** works for the Council for Environmental Education and is also a freelance writer and researcher on environmental issues. She is the author of *Waste and Recycling* and *Conserving the Polar Regions* in Steck-Vaughn's "Conserving Our World" series.

Consultant — **Colin Harris** is the Adviser on Environmental Education for Hertfordshire County Council, England, and an executive member of the Environmental Education Advisers Association.

CONTENTS

Introduction   5

A CHANGING WORLD
The Natural World   6
The Human World   14

PRESSURE ON RESOURCES
Falling Forests   22
Food and Farming   32
Desertification   40
Energy Crisis   48

PROBLEMS OF POLLUTION
Air Pollution   58
Polluted Waters   64

THE FUTURE FOR OUR PLANET
Climate Under Threat   74
Conserving Our World   82

Glossary   92
Further Reading   94
Useful Addresses   94
Index   95

INTRODUCTION

Where does the environment start and where does it end? This is one of those questions that has no answer. After all, we are talking about the whole biosphere — perhaps the whole universe. Everything is a part of the environment. Albert Einstein, the founder of modern nuclear physics, once said that the environment is everything that isn't me; these days it would include him, too.

So an atlas of the environment is a very good way of looking at problems that affect the whole globe.

One important message of this atlas is that, in environmental terms as well as in economic terms, it is the developing world that suffers most. Not only do most poor developing countries owe the rich, developed nations a lot of money, but they are often forced to damage their environment in trying to pay it back.

In making things such as door handles or mahogany toilet seats, the cost is some of the richest habitats on earth, and possibly the extinction of some of the earth's unique species of plant or animal. Perhaps one of the most urgent problems facing the world is to help these nations develop their economies in a way that is good for local communities and does not harm the environment.

Many of the world's surviving tribal peoples, such as the Penans in Malaysia — one of the few who still live by hunting and gathering — are also under threat from the loss of the forests that are their home.

If we were to take a journey into space from the earth's surface, we would first see the environment in the way we see it every day — the city streets and traffic jams, and the huge fields growing, perhaps, a single crop. As we moved further away we could view a district or even a whole country. We would see the polluted oceans, the huge prairies of wheat, the sprawling cities, and the connecting highways cutting deep scars through natural habitats.

From far out in space we could look back and see some of the massive problems that face the earth today, such as the hacking down of the forests and, if we had a special camera, ozone depletion over the polar regions.

We might even see the smogs generated by the cities, the spreading deserts, and the lines made by roads — just some of the evidence of human activity.

Finally we would see a small globe — our planet. We would be looking at a single earth, without boundaries or zones. Perhaps we need to keep all these different views in mind to realize that environmental problems are linked to one another, and to understand how we can start to solve them.

Although the scale of the problems seems huge, it is vital to remember that we all have an important role to play in safeguarding the planet's future — not just how we can benefit the environment by what we do, but also in the influence we have on others. It is actions such as those of women in rural India, who have encouraged tree-planting in their community, that show us a way forward. Your school can play its part by recycling paper, saving energy, or encouraging wildlife.

The best time to begin improving the environment is now, and this atlas is a good place to start. It is full of information to help you understand the problems affecting the world, and how you can help. When you have read it, you might want to become involved with an organization — such as Friends of the Earth — that is fighting to help protect the environment.

The atlas's view of the planet focuses on a range of environmental issues, such as the destruction of habitats, energy use, and air and water pollution. It shows how they are caused and the ways in which the problems are related. For instance, air pollution is connected with transportation issues and energy use. Climate change is being brought about by the way in which we produce our energy, and other issues such as transportation and the destruction of tropical forests.

In the end, both the problems and their solutions depend upon how we look at the earth and the way we fit into it. We need to realize that we are actually a part of the natural world, and that it is not there just for our convenience or for us to destroy.

Left *This view of Earth shows the continent of Africa and the Arabian Peninsula.*

John Howson
Education Officer, Friends of the Earth

THE NATURAL WORLD

Of all the planets in our solar system, life exists only on earth. The surface of Mercury, for example, is far too hot for life to survive, while that of Pluto is far too cold. Only earth has water and an atmosphere to nourish and protect life, and only earth sustains the narrow band of temperatures in which life can thrive.

Life on earth is almost unbelievably varied in its abundance of odd, grotesque, and beautiful forms. There is scarcely a place on the planet that is not inhabited by some living creature. There are bacteria that can live in the fuel tanks of jet planes, and insects that survive in springs that reach 122°F. The young of the brine fly live in almost pure salt, and there are worms that live under the eyelids of hippopotamuses and feed only on their tears. Even in the ice and rocks high above the permanent snow line in the Himalayas, life survives in the form of small insects.

The different climates and landforms of the earth determine where different kinds of vegetation will occur. Types of vegetation are grouped into communities that scientists call biomes. This map shows the earth's main physical features and biomes.

MAJOR BIOMES

- Tundra
- Temperate needleleaf forests
- Temperate broadleaf forests
- Temperate grasslands
- Cold winter deserts
- Mediterranean forests
- Tropical grasslands and savanna
- Warm desert and semi-desert
- Dry tropical forests
- Subtropical and temperate rain forests
- Tropical rain forests
- Mountain areas
- Island systems
- River and lake systems

There may be as many as eight million different species of plants and animals on earth, most still unknown to science. A handful of soil may contain more than a million species of bacteria, as well as 100,000 yeast cells and 50,000 species of fungi. An acre of rich farming soil could contain as many as 120 million small invertebrate creatures, such as mites and millipedes. This teeming multitude of life, among which humans are just one species, exists in a thin layer around the outside of the earth, which scientists call the biosphere.

The Biosphere

The biosphere is the layer of soil, air, and water in which animals and plants live and die. Although earth is one of the smaller planets in the solar system, it measures 3,900 miles from the surface to its center.

Most of the planet consists of the rocks of the mantle and core, much of which are molten.

At 62 miles beneath the surface, the temperature is 5,432°F, far too hot for anything to live.

The atmosphere is estimated to extend 124 miles from the earth's surface, but beyond about 18 miles it is far too cold for any form of life to survive.

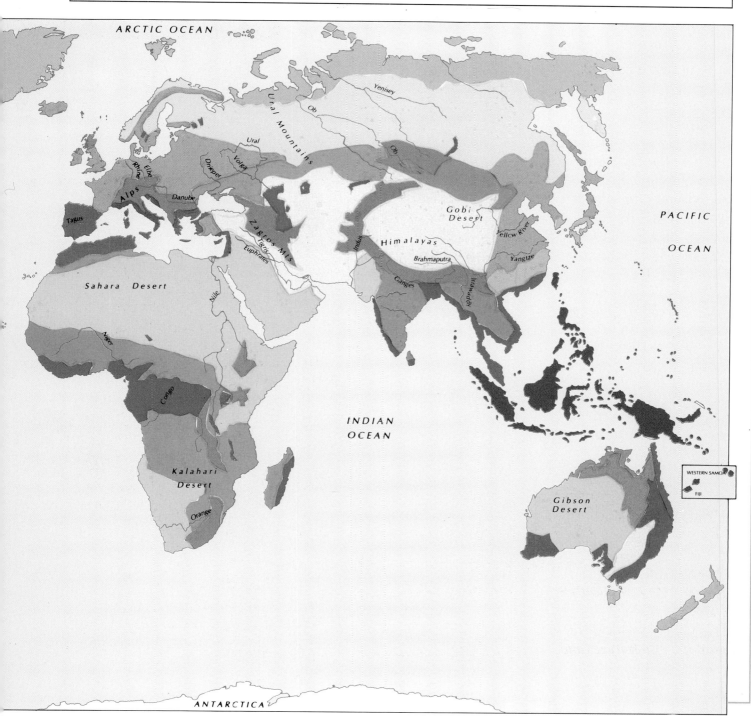

Where did life come from?

Life began on earth around 3.8 billion years ago. Very simple single-celled organisms, similar to bacteria, developed in the warm seas that then covered the planet. Over billions of years these organisms lived, produced new organisms, and died. Slowly they evolved into the enormously complex and diverse system that we know today.

Evolution, the development of species through many small changes over a long period of time, is the process through which this rich diversity of life has developed. New organisms have appeared slowly through natural selection and adaptation.

Throughout the history of the earth the environment has been constantly, if slowly, changing. Life has adapted to these changes, producing many different forms. Successful forms of life survived and produced more offspring; less successful forms became extinct.

Very gradually life became more complicated and diverse. Since life began, many more species have died out than exist in the world today.

The Serengeti

An example of a superbly rich and beautiful ecosystem is the savanna lands that form the Serengeti Plain in Africa. More than half a million animals live on the Serengeti. The savanna teems with life and each species uses a different part of the environment for food. The giraffe with its long neck browses in the tops of the trees. The eland can stand on its hind legs to reach the leaves at the middle level. Smaller species of antelope browse on the lower branches, while the springbok grazes on the grass around the foot of the trees and the warthog unearths roots.

The sun sets over the Serengeti Plain in Africa.

For hundreds of millions of years, life existed only in the ocean. Primitive forms of sea urchins, worms, mollusks, and sponges lived in the forests of seaweed. Plants did not appear on land until 400 million years ago. When the first plants began to emerge from the sea and colonize the land, simple animals like worms followed. Other, more complex animals followed later and eventually evolved into the many different forms of reptiles and amphibians that dominated the earth during the age of dinosaurs. The dinosaurs died out about 70 million years ago, at about the same time that mammals appeared.

The atmosphere of the earth is quite unlike that of other planets. As life evolved, the earth evolved with it. Living organisms released oxygen into the atmosphere, which altered the balance of atmospheric gases and made survival possible.

Left *About 600 million years ago, creatures like this fossilized trilobite were common in the oceans.*

Ecology

As organisms evolved, they interacted with the world around them and with each other to form complex, interdependent ecosystems. All forms of life are interdependent; none can exist in isolation. For example, many animals depend on plants for food and many plants depend on animals to pollinate their flowers. These relationships can become very close and quite complex, as in the case of the ant acacia, a kind of tree that lives in the tropics. Ant acacias have developed large, hollow thorns in which colonies of a particular species of ant live. The trees also provide food for the ants in the form of special structures on the tips of the leaves. In return the ants protect the acacias from other insects and plants.

Without the ants, the trees would be overrun by vines that would strangle them and by other insects that would eat their leaves and burrow into their bark. Both ants and trees benefit from this relationship.

Groups or populations of organisms that occupy the same area, and interchange materials and energy, make up a community. All organisms need energy to survive. Energy flows through an ecosystem in the form of food. Green plants are the producers that turn the energy of sunlight into energy for growth through a process called photosynthesis. Animals cannot produce their own food, so they eat plants and each other. They are called consumers. Decomposers, like fungi and microscopic bacteria, are another important part of the ecosystem. They feed on dead plants and animals and recycle the materials back into the community. These materials then provide fertilizer for the green plants, and the cycle begins again.

In nature each species occupies a different place in its ecosystem, depending on different things for food. This means that each ecosystem can support a great diversity of animals and plants. An organism's place in an ecosystem is called its niche.

The earth's surface

The surface of the earth is far from smooth. Massive forces within the earth have thrown up mighty mountain chains, such as the Himalayas, and the erosive power of water has worn away the land, even carving deep valleys of great beauty, such as the Grand Canyon.

Below *The Grand Canyon has been created over a period of millions of years by the Colorado River wearing away the rocks over which it flows.*

There are mountains and plateaus, mighty rivers like the Amazon, great plains like the Serengeti, deltas and swamps like the Oka-vango in southern Africa, and extraordinary islands like the volcanoes that form the Ha-waiian archipelago. This diversity of land-forms supports an enormous variety of life forms.

The Hawaiian Islands, for example, sup-port an unusual and diverse range of plants and animals. These islands, the most iso-lated in the world, are formed by a chain of volcanoes that rise from the sea floor. There is a great range of types of landscape on these small islands, from beaches to high mountains to lava deserts, but, being so far from other land masses, there are no natu-rally occurring freshwater fish, amphibians, reptiles, or land mammals. This means that other types of animals, such as birds, have occupied the vacant niches. Most plant and animal species that live on the Hawaiian Islands occur nowhere else in the world.

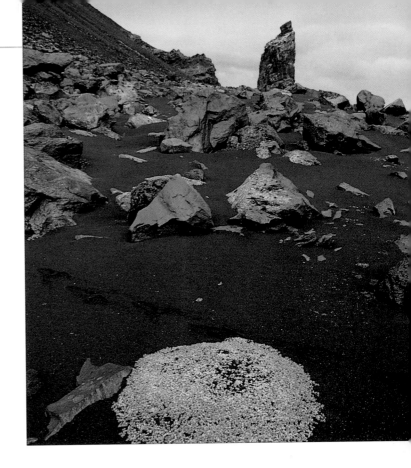

Plants are able to establish themselves in almost any environment — even on recently deposited volcanic lava.

Plants

There are over 300,000 different species of land plants on earth, and they have adapted to almost every environment on this planet, from deserts where it hardly ever rains to the cold Antarctic valleys.

Plants have evolved into extraordinary forms to survive in this broad range of envi-ronments. The welwitschia plant, which lives in the deserts of Namibia in southern Africa, survives for hundreds of years by gathering droplets of fog on two large, leath-ery leaves. In the tropical forests of South-east Asia, there are plants that depend on flies for pollination, attracting them with flowers that look and smell like rotting meat.

A major feature of the earth's surface is the vegetation. Plants make up most of the living matter on this planet. Where different sorts of plants grow depends on the physical factors of light, temperature, the type of soil, and the amount of water available. These physical factors vary according to the cli-

As you go up a mountain, the climate becomes cooler and wetter. As a result, the types of vegetation found at various altitudes can be very different. This diagram shows how vegetation changes with altitude in three areas of the world.

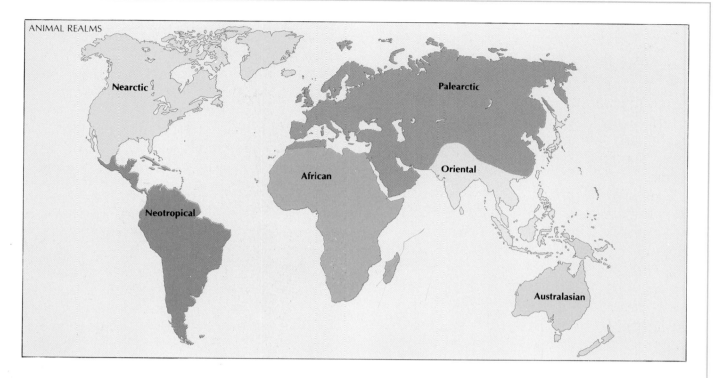

ANIMAL REALMS

Zoologists have divided the world into six realms, based on the similarities between the animals that live in each region.

mate, and the climate varies according to the latitude — where a place lies between the North or South Pole and the equator. Near the equator the climate is hot and wet, while near the poles it is very cold. The temperate regions and the deserts lie between these extremes in climate.

Climate also changes according to altitude. In biological terms, climbing a mountain is somewhat like making a journey toward the poles — the higher you go, the cooler and wetter it usually becomes.

As the climate changes, the vegetation changes. Even in the tropics there are mountains, such as Mt. Kilimanjaro in Tanzania, which have plants that are quite like those in the Arctic. The climatic variations with latitude and altitude mean that vegetation can be classified into broad zones that scientists call biomes. Communities of plants under similar climatic conditions develop along similar lines, and different species often adopt similar forms. The world's principal biomes, including the tundra, temperate grasslands, tropical grasslands, warm and semidesert, are shown on the map on pages 6 and 7.

Animals

Animals inhabit almost every part of the earth's surface. Though the tiger in India is very different from the possum in Australia, and the sloth of South America is very different from the hedgehog of Europe, there are surprising similarities between the groups of animals that inhabit the different continents. In Europe, for example, there are snakes and frogs, butterflies and spiders, earthworms and snails. In Australia, on the other side of the world, you will find the same sorts of animals. They will not be exactly alike but they are clearly from the same animal families.

There are animals living on almost every part of the earth's surface. This bighorn sheep has found itself a precarious perch.

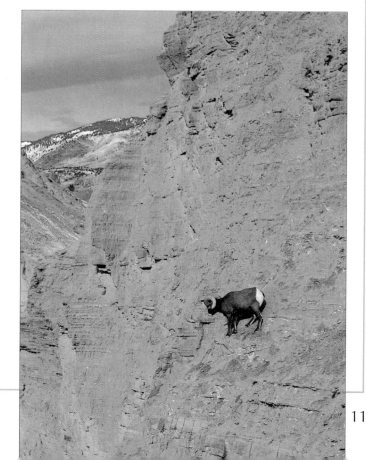

These animals have common ancestors; yet how did they come to be so far apart? Scientists have discovered that continents move very slowly, an inch or two a year. This movement has been going on for hundreds of millions of years and is caused by the same massive forces within the earth that push up mountain chains. Originally all the continents were joined together into one supercontinent called Pangaea, on which early forms of animals, like primitive snakes and frogs, evolved. At various times, some continents split off and began to drift away, carrying with them collections of animals. This movement of continents and islands is often called continental drift.

The different times at which continents broke away from each other and the length of time they have been isolated explains the differences between the animals on different continents. Australia separated from Pangaea very early, and so many of its animals are unique. The marsupials, such as the kangaroo, which carry their young in a pouch, occur almost nowhere else in the world. Scientists have divided the world of animals up into six principal realms, which are shown on the map on page 11.

As continents and islands drifted apart they became isolated from each other, and the animals that inhabited them evolved in different ways. One example is the island of Madagascar, which drifted away from the African continent tens of millions of years ago. Originally it would have had the same groups of animals that then existed in Africa, but they have since evolved into a unique and unusual collection of species. For example, elsewhere in Africa lemurs have been displaced by monkeys and have died out, but there are 25 species of lemur on Madagascar, some of which have only recently been discovered. Half of the world's species of chameleons — small lizards that can change the color of their skin to match that of their surroundings — live on the island of Madagascar.

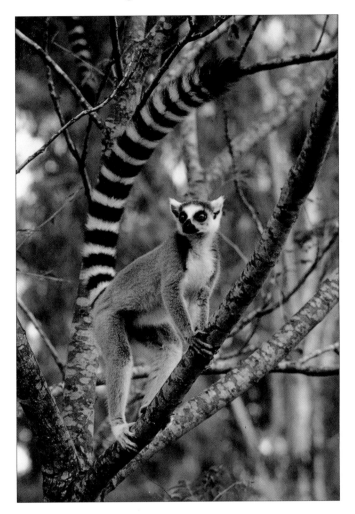

Above *Lemurs live only on the island of Madagascar.*

Left *A deep-sea angler fish waits to attract prey with its glowing lure.*

WORLD MAP OF SEA-BED

East Pacific Rise · *Peru-Chile Trench* · *Mid-Atlantic Ridge* · *Mid-Indian Ridge* · *Marianas Trench* · *Tonga Trench* · *Pacific-Antarctic Ridge*

Left *It was once thought that the seabed was a flat, featureless plain, but scientists have found that there are mountain ranges, deep trenches, cliffs, and plateaus.*

Below *Emperor penguins on the ice of Antarctica — the world's last great wilderness*

The Oceans

Over 70 percent of our planet's surface is covered by oceans and seas. Earth is the only planet in our solar system that has large areas covered by water; the other planets are too hot or too cold and any water that existed has either frozen or evaporated. It is water that makes life possible on earth, and the oceans are home to a huge number of plant and animal species.

Life in the sea is divided into zones that are based on depth. There is the tidal zone, where the sea meets the land. Next there are the shallow continental shelves that surround the land masses. Most life in the sea lives in these two shallowest zones because there is plentiful light for photosynthesis. Beyond the continental shelf in the ocean basins there are two more zones, one of light and another of perpetual darkness. Light does not pass very well through water, and the darkness increases with depth. Below about 650 feet light does not penetrate at all and it is always dark.

Extraordinary life forms inhabit the ocean depths. Giant squid live at 1,500 feet, and sometimes sperm whales will dive down to these depths to eat the squid. As there is no light in the depths, there are no plants that produce food by means of photosynthesis. Therefore, the organisms that live here must depend on debris that falls from above for their food, or prey on each other. The angler fish has a permanent lure that projects from its forehead, almost like a fishing rod. It has a lighted tip that hangs in front of its mouth.

Small fish are attracted to this luminous or glowing tip in the dark of the ocean depths and are eaten by the angler fish. The lantern fish also has organs that give off light under water.

Wilderness

Wilderness is the natural world in its original, unaltered state. It is the part of the earth's surface that is uncultivated or uninhabited by humans. In fact, in many places that are considered to be wilderness there are people living, whether it is the Yanomami Indians in the Amazon rain forest or the Eskimos on the tundra in Alaska. Wilderness is very important, since it preserves the diversity of nature as a living functioning whole.

There are a few places left that are wilderness in the sense of being uninhabited. Antarctica is, perhaps, the last great wilderness, and even this frozen continent is threatened by human interference.

THE HUMAN WORLD

If you could view the earth from deep space, you would not see the effect of people on the planet. But in this century, people have had more effect on the global environment than they have done in the previous millions of years of human history.

Part of the reason for this big effect is the large increase in the number of people on earth. Today, there are over 5.2 billion people. Each day, another quarter of a million people are added to the population.

This population has grown rapidly over the last 200 years, and although growth rates are now slowing down, they may

not reach equilibrium for another 100 years or so.

The world map below shows how quickly the populations of the countries of the world are growing. Although the percentage increase figures may seem small, the populations of certain countries grow quickly. For example, a four percent increase each year

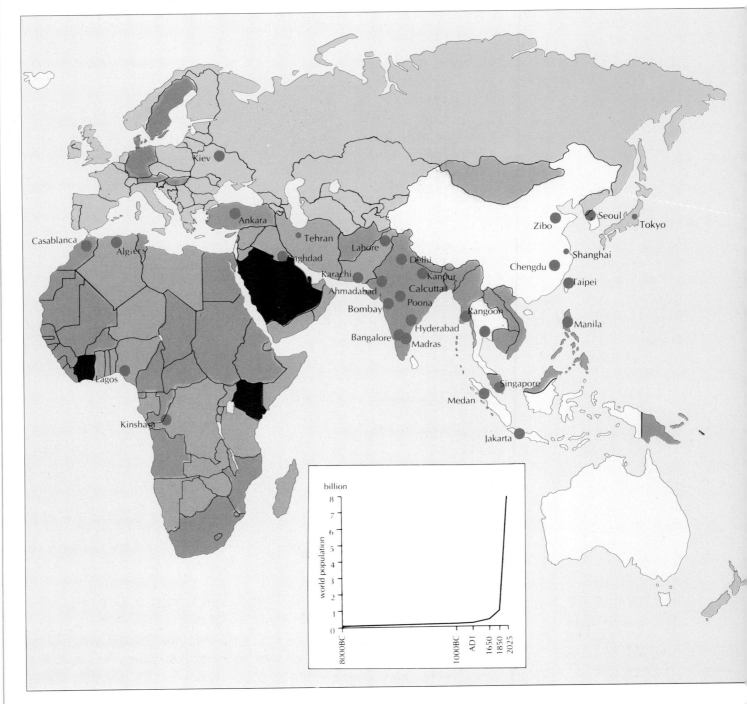

means that a country's population will double in just over 17 years.

People on earth

For many thousands of years, the number of people on earth has increased only very gradually. The graph on page 14 shows how the level of population was fairly even until about the year 1600; since then the rate of increase has quickened.

The estimated world population in 8000 B.C. was only about 5 million people — about twice as large as the population of Washington, D.C. today. By A.D. 1, it was about 150 million and by 1650, it had reached 500 million. It then took 200 years to double to 1,000 million (1 billion), and

only about 80 years to double again to 2 billion by the 1930s. By 1975, just 45 years later, it had reached 4 billion, and is expected to top 8 billion by the year 2025.

Above *A home for elderly people in Germany. In developed countries people live longer than in developing countries, because they are wealthier and health care is better.*

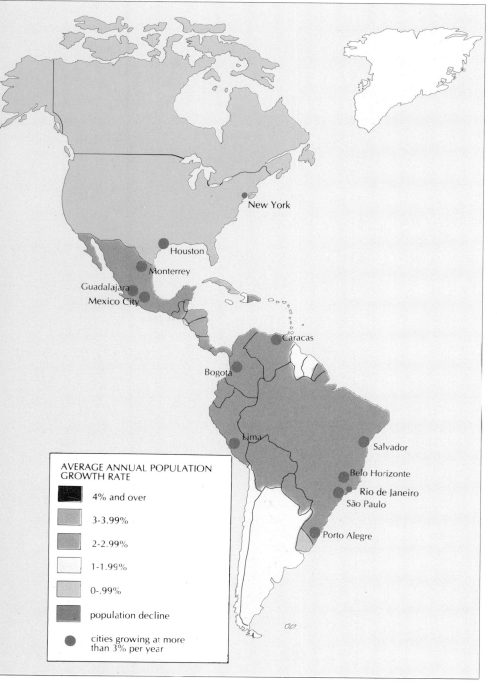

AVERAGE ANNUAL POPULATION GROWTH RATE

- 4% and over
- 3-3.99%
- 2-2.99%
- 1-1.99%
- 0-.99%
- population decline
- cities growing at more than 3% per year

This map shows how fast the population is increasing in different countries and highlights the fastest-growing cities. The cities named on the map are all fast growing. Those that will be the world's largest in the year 2000 are: Tehran, Calcutta, Bombay, Shanghai, Seoul, Tokyo, Mexico City, New York, Rio de Janeiro, and São Paulo.

These growth-rate figures do not tell the whole story; China has a relatively low growth rate but, because it has a huge number of people, its population increased by over 13.6 million between 1985 and 1990.

The rapid rise in world population began in the first countries to industrialize — those in Western Europe especially. The growth or decline in any population depends on the birth rate and the death rate. If, each year, around the same number of people are born as the number that die, the total population stays at the same level. But, beginning in the seventeenth century, people began to live longer as health and food supplies improved. Eventually, in developed countries, increasing prosperity led to a lowering of the birth rate. Today the population in the developed countries is growing very slowly or declining.

About 90 percent of the increase in world population is now in the developing countries. Since the 1940s, the death rate has fallen in most developing countries, mostly through control of disease. At the same time, the birth rate has risen. Together, these two trends have resulted in rapidly increasing populations in most countries in the developing world.

For couples in the developing world, there are good reasons for having many children. Most people are very poor by Western standards, and there are normally very few health and social services provided, particularly in rural areas. So children are seen as an investment — they are able to work and bring in income for the family and provide help and security for parents in their old age. But parents feel they need to have many children as insurance. Worldwide over 14 million children die before the age of 5, and most of these are in the developing world.

Although birth rates are beginning to fall in many developing countries, they are still high. World population may not stop rising until the year 2100, by which time it may have reached 14 billion. This would put great strain on the resources and life-support systems of the planet, such as the soil, water, and atmosphere. It may be possible to prevent the population from reaching such a high figure, but that depends on action taken today.

The most effective way of tackling high birth rates is to improve people's lives. Making birth control more widely available is part of the solution, but fighting poverty, providing better health care and education,

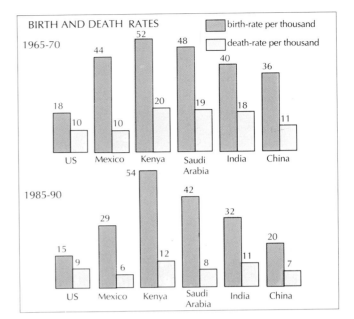

A country's population grows when the birth rate is higher than the death rate.

and raising the status of women in developing countries are more effective in reducing the number of children born.

The city people
More and more people are living in cities. At the beginning of this century only around ten percent of the world's population lived in cities, but by the year 2000 nearly half will live in an urban area.

As with population growth, the increase in the size of cities began first in the industrialized countries. The Industrial Revolution of the eighteenth and nineteenth centuries led to the growth of major cities in the Western countries. By 1960, six out of the ten largest cities in the world were located in these industrialized countries. But by the year 2000, only two such cities — Tokyo and New York — will be in this top ten list of cities; the other eight will be in developing nations.

The giant cities of the developing world are growing much faster than the cities in the developed world have ever done. One reason for this growth is population increase; the other is the migration of people from rural areas to towns and cities.

Right *The proportion of the population living in cities is growing in many parts of the world, but especially in developing countries. By the year 2000, most of the world's largest cities will be in developing nations.*

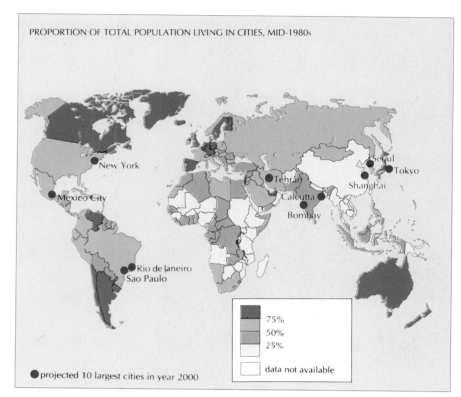

PROPORTION OF TOTAL POPULATION LIVING IN CITIES, MID-1980s

New York
Mexico City
Tehran
Seoul
Tokyo
Shanghai
Calcutta
Bombay
Rio de Janeiro
Sao Paulo

75%
50%
25%
data not available

● projected 10 largest cities in year 2000

Below *This village in Burkina Faso, West Africa, is now deserted. Its people have moved away in the hope of finding a better life in the city.*

Two different forces combine to cause people to migrate to cities. These are forces that "push" people from the land and others that "pull" them toward the cities. Some examples of push factors are the difficulty of making a living in rural areas; infertile land; lack of wood for fuel; the replacement of food farming with growing crops for export; loss of vital jobs to increasing mechanization; and in some places famine or war.

The pull factors that attract people to the cities include the chance of a job, help from relatives in the city, cheaper food, and more chance of health care and education. The city offers many attractions, yet the problems supporting oneself and a family in an urban environment are very difficult ones.

Migration is resulting in the growth of large shanty towns or slums around most of the big cities in the developing world. Some of these squatter settlements are so large they form areas the size of cities themselves. Because the people are poor, they have to squat on the poorest land, which is often unfit for housing. It may suffer from flooding, be situated on a hillside, or next to polluting industry or the city dump. There may be no services — water, electricity, garbage collection, or sewers — but the people have no place to go. Often they are resourceful and can improve their settlements over time, but the pressure of new arrivals makes lasting improvement difficult.

The rapid growth of cities in developing countries puts pressure on the environment, particularly through air and water pollution. Poor urban dwellers are often the first to suffer the effects of this pollution. To confront these problems, city and national governments need to help the squatter settlements by providing basic services. They also have to reduce migration to the cities by tackling poverty in the rural areas.

This shanty town outside Manila, the capital of the Philippines, is built on top of a garbage dump.

Many cities in developed countries are also facing problems. Air pollution, noise, and traffic congestion are common problems in all large cities. But unlike the cities in the developing world, cities in the developed world can more easily afford to solve their problems.

Rich world, poor world
Many people point to the world's growing population as the reason for our environmental problems. However, although population size is important, the way in which resources are used by different groups of people is also crucial.

The environment is being damaged by

Above *Hong Kong citizens at a cash machine. In all countries there are poor people and others who are comparatively rich.*

extremes of wealth and poverty within countries, but more particularly between countries. Less than a quarter of the world's population (about 1.2 billion people) lives in the developed nations, but they consume three-quarters of the world's resources and enjoy two-thirds of the world's income. This unequal sharing of resources is perpetuated

Below *This map shows the wealth of countries, in terms of each country's gross national product per capita — the total value of the goods and services it produces in a year divided by its population.*

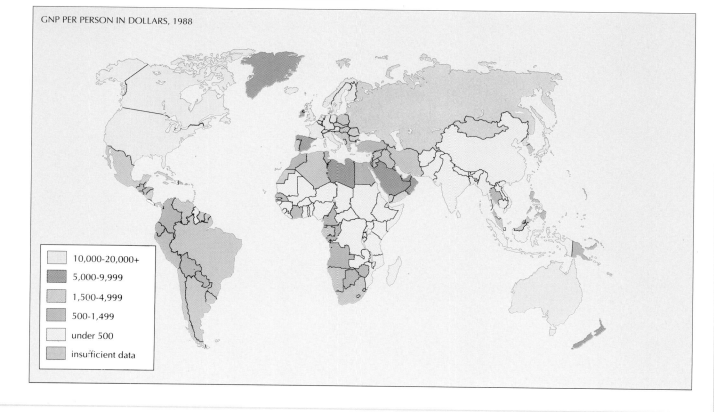

GNP PER PERSON IN DOLLARS, 1988

- 10,000-20,000+
- 5,000-9,999
- 1,500-4,999
- 500-1,499
- under 500
- insufficient data

by the richer nations who depend on the raw materials produced in developing countries — such as metal ores, textiles, and food materials — to maintain their wealthy, industrialized economies.

Unfortunately, the developing nations do not get a fair price for their goods or commodities. The richer countries are able to control the market prices, and in the 1980s many of the commodity prices dropped. Meanwhile, the prices of the manufactured goods and oil that the developing countries need to buy have risen. This means the terms of trade are in the developed countries' favor.

This problem is made worse by the debt crisis. In the 1970s many developing countries borrowed money from the developed countries and Western banks to finance development projects, such as dams and industrial plants. They had to pay interest on the loans, before long interest rates went up steeply, partly as a result of the oil crisis. By the 1980s many countries were having difficulty paying the interest.

Some countries, such as Brazil, Mexico, and Argentina, have increased the area of land devoted to "cash crops" for export to try and earn more money. This leaves less land available for the rural poor, who have in turn been forced to overgraze their land,

resulting in soil erosion and migration to the cities. At the same time, the debt crisis has meant that developing countries have had little money available to improve basic services such as clean water, housing, health and education — which would help reduce the birth rate. They have also had few funds for protecting the environment.

In global terms, the debt crisis and unequal trade terms mean that the poorer countries lose more to the richer countries than they gain from them. The developing nations pay out over $50 billion a year more than they receive in new loans or aid from the developed countries. Over the last few decades, the rich countries have been getting richer while the poor have become poorer.

This situation also applies to the sharing of wealth within countries. In the developed world increasing numbers of people are living on income support — money provided by governments to help those with low incomes. But in most cities in developing countries the extremes of poverty and wealth are greater and more visible. About a quarter of the world's population now lives

This plantation in the Philippines grows pineapples as a cash crop. The fruit is exported to richer countries.

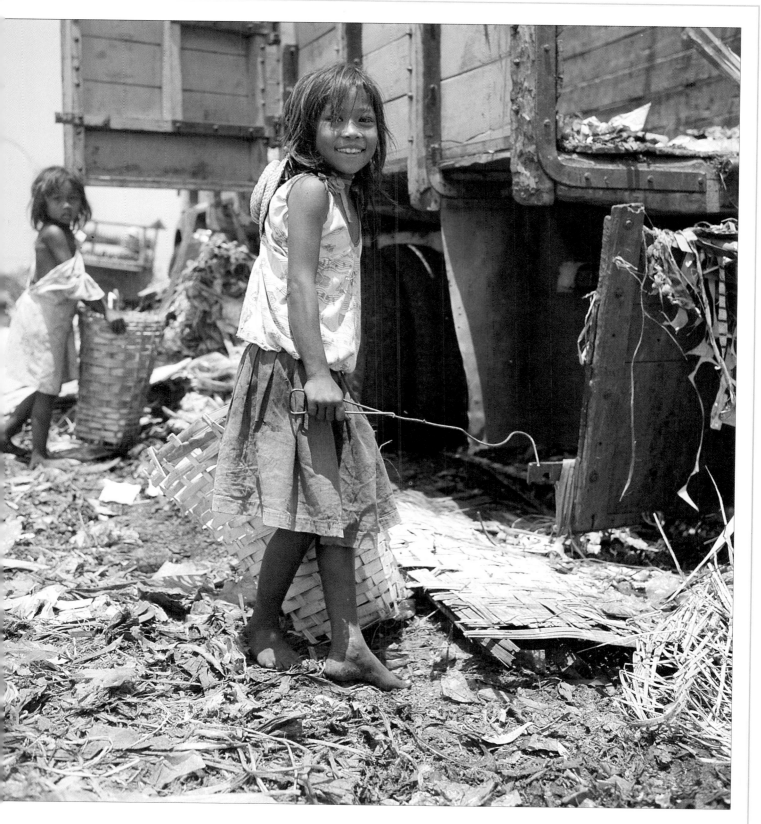

These children in Jakarta, the capital of Indonesia, are scavenging in the garbage for anything that they might be able to sell.

in deep poverty.

The earth's resources are limited. This means that they have to be shared much more equally and used much more carefully. Resources, such as coal, gas, minerals, water, and even fertile soil, need to be used carefully if future generations are to be able to meet their needs. The idea of sustainable development, which tries to develop economic activity that does not harm the local or global ecological balance, is gaining sup-

port. It involves recycling, the efficient use of energy and resources, and keeping waste to a minimum. In developing countries, in particular, it means creating projects that are based on people's real needs, and that protect rather than destroy the local culture and ecology.

FALLING FORESTS

Forests are much more than collections of trees. They are the
natural vegetation of over 40 percent of the earth's land surface
and include some of the most complex ecosystems on the planet.
There are many different types of forest. Each is made up of
different kinds of trees and has a whole range of plant and animal
life adapted to living within it. Although the same general type of
forest can be found in different continents, each contains its own
unique species. So if a forest in one part of the world is damaged
or destroyed, many forms of life may disappear forever from
the face of the earth.

*This map shows the world's
forest and woodland areas.
What type of forest grows in a
particular area depends upon
the climate and the kind of soil
that is present. The inset picture shows the trees that are
most commonly found in certain types of forests.*

ATLANTIC
OCEAN

PACIFIC
OCEAN

Taiga

Temperate forest

Tropical
forest

Life in the rain forest

Tropical rain forests are made up of several layers. Each layer has its own world of plants and animals that all depend on each other. The trees depend on animals to pollinate them and spread their seeds, and the animals depend on trees for their food and shelter.

The highest layer in a rain forest is the canopy, over 100 feet above the ground, formed by the crowns of tall trees. The canopy has more life than any other part of the forest because it receives most of the rain and sunlight. The trees flower and produce fruit all year round, providing food for birds, insects, bats, and monkeys. Other animals, including some squirrels, lizards, frogs, and even snakes, are specially adapted to spend their whole lives in the treetops.

Up to 50 feet above the ground smaller trees, such as palms or young saplings, form another layer — the understory. Here it is quiet and humid. The leaves provide food for a few large mammals, like deer, okapi, and tapirs. These animals are hunted by carnivores.

On the forest floor the light is very dim. Only a few plants that can survive in the shade live there. Fallen leaves, dead branches, and even tree trunks decay very rapidly in these hot, damp surroundings due to multitudes of fungi, insects, and other organisms that feed on decomposing matter. The minerals yielded by decaying trees are taken up again by the living trees' shallow roots, so a good deal of the material is quickly recycled before it can be washed away by rain.

FOREST AREAS

Temperate needleleaf forests and woodlands (taiga)

Temperate broadleaf forests and woodlands

Sub-tropical and temperate rain forests and woodlands

Tropical rain forests

Dry tropical forests

Mediterranean forests, scrub and woodlands

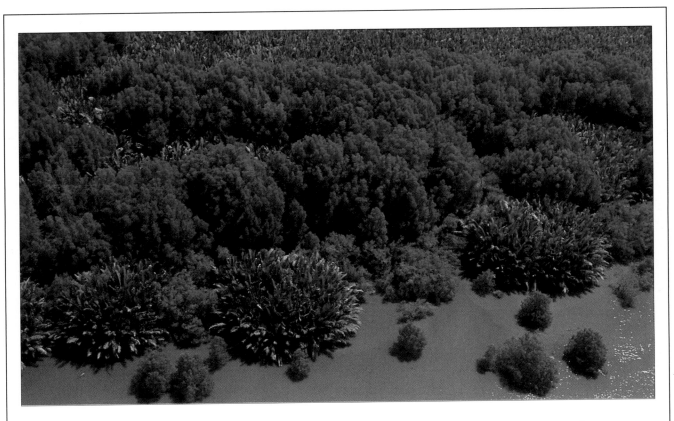

Different Kinds of Forest

The forests of northern Canada and Russia are known as **taiga.** They have evergreen coniferous trees like pines, spruces, and firs. Here the winters are long and intensely cold, rainfall is low, and the soils are poor and sandy. These conifers provide "softwood" which is made into paper for printing, packaging, and babies' diapers, in addition to plywood and wood for building houses and making pine furniture.

In the middle latitudes, where the temperature is above 50°F for at least half the year and the annual rainfall is over 15 inches, **broad-leaved deciduous forests** are the natural vegetation. In Europe these forests contain oaks, beeches, birches, lindens, chestnuts, and elms. In the U.S. maples and hickories are also common woodlands trees. Much of these forests has been cleared over the last 2,000 years to make room for farming and places for people to live.

Farther south, particularly on eastern continental coasts where there is less danger of frost, there are broad-leaved evergreen forests, also known as **temperate rain forest.** They are made up of trees called southern beeches, and conifers like the kauri pine or the chile pine tree.

Tropical rain forests are found in countries all along the equator but occur mainly in three great blocks — Amazonia, the Congo, and Southeast Asia. In these areas the tem-

An aerial view of mangrove trees and nipa palms in Brunei, Southeast Asia. Mangroves grow in tropical climates, usually along riverbanks.

perature and rainfall are high all year round. Thousands of different types of plants grow in tropical rain forests, including creepers, climbers, and ferns, but the most important are the huge evergreen trees that form the forest canopy. Tropical rain forests are vanishing fast due to logging, burning, and mining by developers, settlers, and farmers.

Where there is an annual dry season, **dry tropical forest** may form the natural vegetation. There are several different types, including the monsoon forests of India and Myanmar where teak is important, and the savanna woodland of Africa where acacia trees are common. These forests are in even greater danger than rain forests as people clear the land for cattle grazing or cut the trees for firewood.

Where the summers are hot and dry, and the winters warm and wet, what is known as **Mediterranean forest** — another kind of evergreen forest — grows, made up of evergreen oaks and other plants with small, tough leaves that can withstand drought. Eucalyptus forests in Australia are similar. Much of this type of forest has been destroyed by forest fires and the development of tourist resorts along the coasts.

The removal of just one forest tree, even by natural causes, affects all the plants around it. Some of the shade-loving plants in lower layers may die in the fierce light and heat of the sun. Other seedlings, unable to grow in the shade, shoot up and eventually close the gap in the canopy. Where trees are felled the forest cannot easily grow back. When a tree is cut down, as many as 20 others may be seriously damaged as it falls or by the machinery used to take it away. Once a large patch of the forest floor is laid bare, the heavy tropical rains wash away the minerals, seeds, and even the dark brown soil.

The wealth of plant life in rain forests has misled people to think these areas would be ideal for farmland. In fact, the soil is usually very poor. After two or three seasons of growing crops like corn or coffee the land is so infertile that only sparse, coarse grass can grow on it.

Why forests are important to people

Trees provided shelter, firewood, tools, and food for the first humans. As society developed, some forests were cleared to grow crops. Wood was cut from forests for buildings and tools or to make charcoal for smelting metals. The remaining forest was left as hunting grounds and as places where people could collect fruits, nuts, fungi, honey, and other forest products for food and for medicines.

Forests have also been linked to magic or religious beliefs. Even today, people regard forests — or their remnants, woods — with a sense of wonder and pleasure. Many millions of people all over the world still depend on forests for their living — through tourism as well as logging, hunting, and gathering.

Lush vegetation in the rain forest of Costa Rica, Central America

Forests are also important to people in less obvious ways. They help to keep the balance of nature in the air, water, and soil. Trees and other plants use the energy in sunlight to take carbon dioxide from the air. With it they form sugars and other substances that make up the body of the plant. In this process, which is called photosynthesis, they give out oxygen. Like all other living things, plants respire to release energy to grow. As a result, carbon dioxide goes back into the atmosphere. The carbon trapped in plants is also released as carbon dioxide when plants are burned or when they die.

Some scientists fear that the rapid destruction of forests, particularly the burning of tropical forests, is adding to the "greenhouse effect." The large amounts of carbon dioxide produced by burning trees enter the atmosphere, adding to the layer of gases that are already there. These gases act like the glass roof of a greenhouse — allowing sunlight to enter and trapping some of the sun's heat. If some heat were not trapped by the atmosphere, the earth would be far too cold for living things to exist. However, if there are too many greenhouse gases, too much heat will be trapped.

There is growing concern that this could cause global warming, which might have a dramatic effect on the world climate, but there is no clear evidence yet.

There is, however, evidence to show that forests affect local climates. Trees and plants take up water

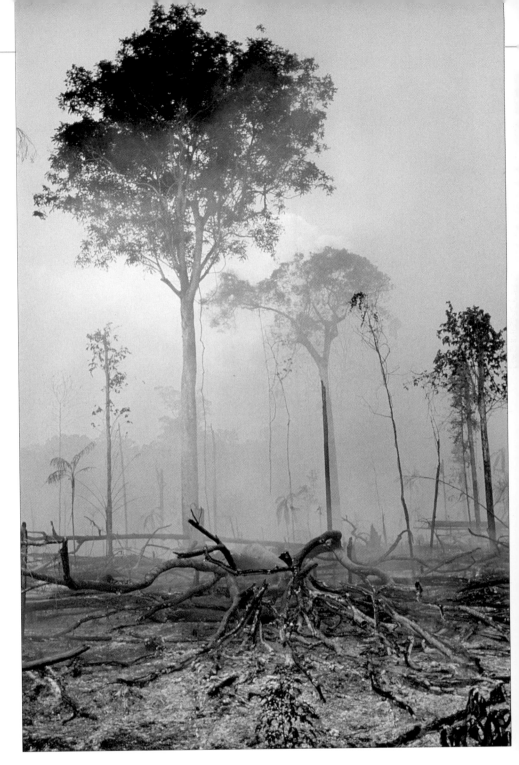

This area of rain forest in Brazil is being cleared so that the land can be used for agriculture. The soil is not very fertile and will be useless for farming or grazing in two to three years.

through their roots and lose it through their leaves. That is why the air in and around forests is always moist. In hot tropical regions such large amounts of water are lost from the trees that clouds form above the forest. The rain that falls is then absorbed by tree roots, and the whole cycle begins over again.

Trees also prevent soil erosion. Their roots bind the soil together and help to prevent it from being washed away. Their leaves and branches break the force of heavy rains and protect the soil surface, allowing the water to trickle or drip down. In this way forests act as giant sponges, soaking up water and allowing any excess to flow gently downhill.

tropical rain forests.

European forests are fairly young. Until the end of the last ice age, about 10,000 years ago, huge areas of the earth, including much of Europe, were covered with great ice sheets. Glaciers were formed at this time.

A few acres of temperate woodland have about 40 different kinds of trees or shrubs. In the same sized area of tropical rain forest, 200 different sorts of trees may grow. Each type of tree has many hundreds of animals — mammals, reptiles, birds, and insects — living on or close to it.

Above *Deforestation caused this landslide in Malaysia. In the background a truck carries away more felled trees.*

Below *Forests are home to many species of plants and animals.*

In northern regions, including parts of Canada and the European Alps, evergreen forests on mountainsides help protect the villages below from avalanches. In tropical climates, where the rainfall is often sudden and very heavy, forest-covered slopes prevent flooding and mudslides that could cause death and damage to millions of people living in the valleys. Forests on hills and mountainsides also stop the soils of fertile farmland from being washed away.

Forests as wildlife reservoirs

Forests are important as home to millions of species of plants and animals. The forests that are richest in plant and animal life are found at the equator, where the climate has stayed the same for millions of years. The first flowering plants may have evolved in these

Left *This map shows the vanishing rain forest of Southeast Asia. By the year 2000, Thailand will have lost 60 percent of the tropical forest it had in 1981.*

Right *Logs are floated downstream to a wood-pulp mill in Quebec province, Canada.*

Below *The construction of a new road cuts a deep scar through the Amazon rain forest.*

TROPICAL RAIN FORESTS IN SOUTHEAST ASIA

tropical forests in late 1980s

forests lost since 1940

Conservationists are concerned about the destruction of all forests, but especially tropical rain forests, because so many types of plants and animals live there. Only seven percent of the earth's surface is covered by tropical forests, yet they contain more than half the species found on this planet. Most of these will vanish with the forests, in many cases before scientists have had a chance to find out anything about them.

Some plants from tropical forests are useful for medicines, for the local people and for modern medicine. For example, quinine — a drug used to treat malaria comes from the bark of a tropical tree. The rosy periwinkle from the forests of Madagascar is used to make a drug that combats a form of cancer in children.

Other forest plants are relatives of crops that we use for food, such as bananas, oranges, and coffee. These wild plants are needed to help develop new varieties that produce more food and are more resistant to diseases.

The vanishing forests

Scientists cannot agree on how fast or how seriously people are damaging and destroying forests. However, they do agree that forests are vanishing rapidly and, year by year, the forest that remains is disappearing even faster.

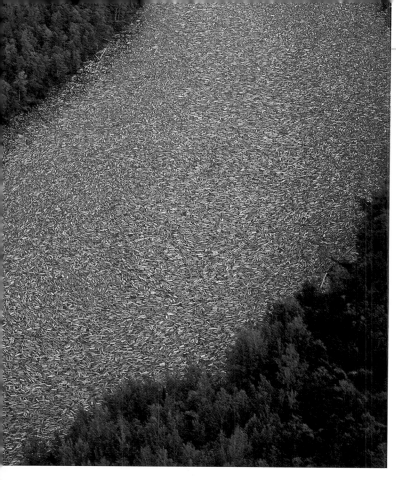

As much as 50 million acres of tropical forest may be destroyed or damaged each year. This means that up to 95 acres may be destroyed every minute. About half the world's tropical rain forests have disappeared in the last 50 years. At the present rate much of what is left could be damaged beyond repair by the year 2000.

In the past, logging methods were not as destructive to forests as they are today. It took two men more than a day to fell a tropical hardwood tree with axes and handsaws. Elephants or buffalo then pulled the timber to logging camps and the logs were floated down rivers. Today one man can fell many trees in a day using a chain saw. Giant tractors drag the trunks to depots where trucks take them to towns and ports.

There are many reasons why forests are destroyed, but the most important is money. Governments in tropical countries allow logging companies to cut down trees as a quick way of obtaining money for their countries' needs. They need to pay for schools, hospitals, clean water, and housing for their growing populations, or to pay back money borrowed from wealthier countries. Over one-third of the tropical timber felled is shipped to Europe, which is the second most important timber market in the world after Japan. Raw wood and chipboard, which were once huge tropical trees, are made into all types of furniture, doors, and even toilet seats!

Roads made by logging companies open up the forests to settlers. In many countries, especially in Latin America and Southeast Asia, most of the best farmland is owned by a few rich people, and millions of poor people have no land at all. Poor families often move to forest areas and clear the land to grow food. Sometimes the government encourages them to do this rather than move to overcrowded cities.

Tropical forests are often cut down to make plantations of so-called "cash crops," such as tea, coffee, tobacco, sugar, cotton, and palm oil. The plantations provide work for thousands of people, and the country gets money by exporting the cash crops to rich countries overseas. In Central and South America forests have been burned to make grassland for cattle; much of the meat produced is sold abroad.

Some governments, international banks, and overseas aid agencies like the World Bank have lent money to developing countries for projects that destroy rain forests. These include building hydroelectric dams, mining, cash crop farming, plantations, and cattle ranching. Many of these projects fail, but the country still has to repay the loan.

About 2 billion people use wood to cook food, boil water, and keep themselves warm. Rapid population growth and increasing poverty mean people are cutting down trees faster than they can be replaced. This is one of the main threats to the drier tropical forests of Africa and Asia.

It is not only tropical forests that are endangered, however. In temperate regions trees are also under threat. Around 2,000 years ago, most of northern Europe was covered with forests. Today what little forest remains is mostly in national parks or protected areas. The rest has been cleared to grow crops, graze animals, provide places for people to live and work, or to mine the minerals beneath the surface. Even what is left of the temperate forests is not safe. Millions of acres of trees throughout Europe may be suffering from the effects of acid rain which often includes sulfur dioxide, nitrogen oxides, and hydrocarbons. (See pp. 58 – 60.)

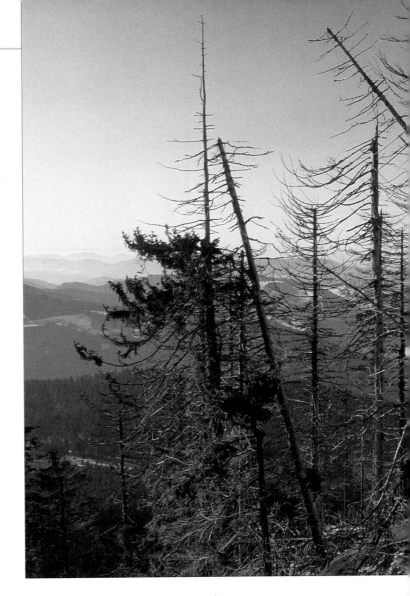

Above *Trees killed by acid rain in Germany's Black Forest*

Paying the Price

- In Thailand, more than 350 people were killed in November 1988 when villages were washed away by floods. The forests on the hills had been cut down for timber and to make fields to grow crops.
- In Sarawak, Malaysia, many Penans — one of the last forest people in the world — have been arrested for blockading logging roads. They are protesting that timber companies are destroying their way of life. Fishing, game, sago, rattan, and other forest products have all become scarce since the loggers opened up the area.
- In 1983 a fire that started in Kalimantan, Indonesia, destroyed an area of swamp forest bigger than Belgium. Two years later the peaty soil was still smoldering. It is not known how the fire started, but dead wood left behind by loggers helped it spread out of control.
- Nine iron smelters and two cement factories are planned in the Amazon forest of Brazil. Funds for the Grande Carajas Program have come mainly from the European Community (EC). At least 3.7 million acres of forest will be cut down to make charcoal for these industries. The survival of 27 tribes of Indians who live there is threatened.
- The lakes that supply water to the Panama Canal in Central America are slowly filling up with soil washed down from the surrounding hills. The forests there have been cleared by poor farmers who have moved up to the hillsides because richer farmers have taken the better land. If this continues there will not be enough water for large ships to pass through the locks in the canal.
- Severe flooding in Bangladesh affected 85 percent of the country in 1988. In the past, when the lower Himalayas were covered with trees, flood disasters only happened twice a century. By the 1970s terrible floods were happening every four years.

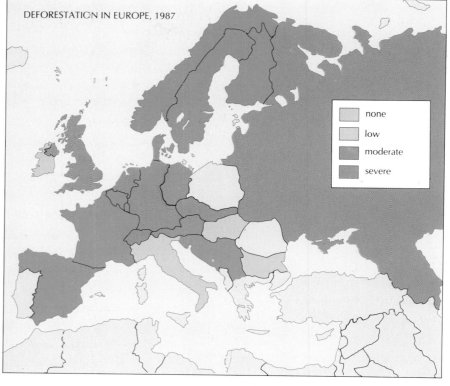

DEFORESTATION IN EUROPE, 1987

none
low
moderate
severe

Below *Deforested land being used for cattle ranching in Brazil. Some of the beef produced will be sold abroad to be made into hamburgers.*

Above *Deforestation does not affect tropical rain forests alone. As this map shows, the remaining temperate forests of Europe are also being destroyed.*

Organizations like the World Wide Fund for Nature and Friends of the Earth can put pressure on governments to protect forests by setting up national parks and nature reserves. They also raise money for the preservation of these forests and perform scientific research.

However, we cannot protect all the world's remaining forests this way. The best way is to encourage people to use only small parts of the forests to make money without cutting them down. Some temperate forests can be used carefully to provide timber. Tropical forests produce far more than just wood; nuts, oils, spices, dyes, fish, and game can all be harvested without harming the forests. Forest people have been doing this for thousands of years.

We can help by trying to use wood from plantations or specially managed projects where trees are replanted to replace those that have been cut down. If people in rich countries were to stop buying timber and furniture made from tropical rain forest hardwood trees, like teak and mahogany, logging would decrease.

Saving the forests

There are many reasons why forests are being damaged and destroyed in the world, and no easy solutions to the problem. Everyone has to share the responsibility — governments, organizations, and individuals.

FOOD AND FARMING

Today 5.2 billion people must share the food resources of the globe. By the year 2000 there will be an extra billion mouths to feed, and experts estimate we will need 40 percent more food than we already grow. During the last 50 years, intensive farming methods — using machines, fertilizers, and pesticides — have been used to increase crop yields. However, these methods carry a huge environmental cost. In many areas over-use of farmland has destroyed the fertility of the soil, chemicals have polluted the land, and waste from livestock farming has poisoned the water. Wildlife habitats have also been destroyed in the quest to increase the amount of land under cultivation. If these problems are to be avoided in the future, we will have to find new ways of growing food that will put back into the earth as much as we take out, if not more. Otherwise hunger and famine will only increase.

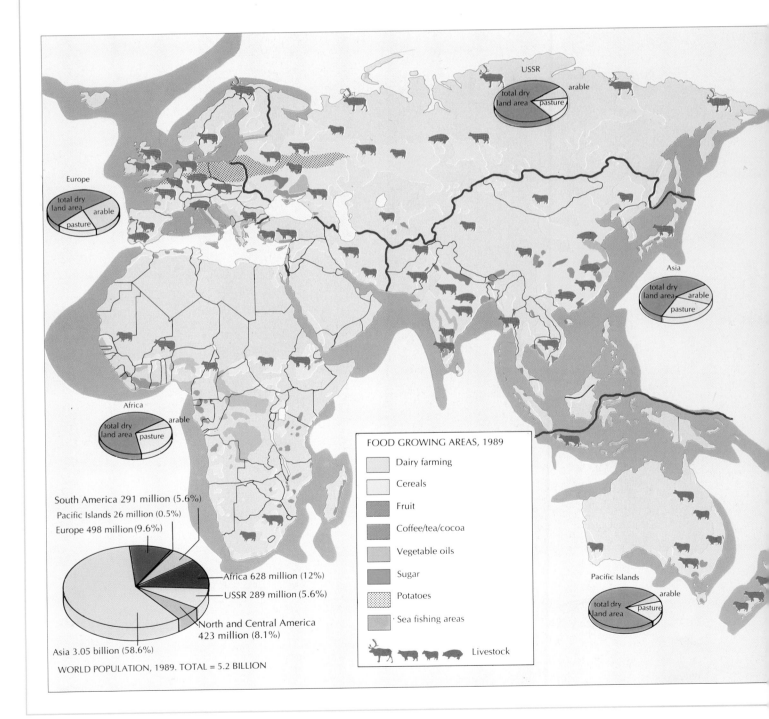

USSR
total dry land area   arable
pasture

Europe
total dry land area   arable
pasture

Asia
total dry land area   arable
pasture

Africa
total dry land area   arable
pasture

Pacific Islands
total dry land area   arable
pasture

FOOD GROWING AREAS, 1989

Dairy farming

Cereals

Fruit

Coffee/tea/cocoa

Vegetable oils

Sugar

Potatoes

Sea fishing areas

Livestock

South America 291 million (5.6%)
Pacific Islands 26 million (0.5%)
Europe 498 million (9.6%)
Africa 628 million (12%)
USSR 289 million (5.6%)
North and Central America 423 million (8.1%)
Asia 3.05 billion (58.6%)

WORLD POPULATION, 1989. TOTAL = 5.2 BILLION

How agriculture began

Early humans fed themselves by hunting wild animals and gathering plants, nuts, and fruits. Agriculture, or the cultivation of soil, first developed around 10,000 years ago when people started to grow food crops on the fertile floodplains and deltas of various rivers, such as the Nile in Egypt, the Yangtze in China, and the Tigris and Euphrates in Mesopotamia.

These first farmers selected wild plants and developed ways to grow and harvest them as foodstuffs. Later, in steep and hilly areas, farmers built level terraces on the slopes to make the land easier to cultivate. In drier areas they constructed dams and channels to capture precious water and deliver it to the fields. In some places people have practiced shifting cultivation for centuries, moving on every few years to clear a new plot of land.

Land use and soil fertility

Today we cultivate 11 percent of the total dry area of the globe. Some experts say we could double this, but others doubt that many of the unused areas are fertile enough to grow crops.

The distribution of soil fertility is very uneven. For instance, in Europe fertile soils cover more than 36 percent of the land area; more than 80 percent of these good soils are cultivated. In hot, wet, tropical regions soil fertility is far more fragile because torrential rains wash away most of the nutrients. In the rain forest a small plot of land

North and Central America

total dry land area — arable — pasture

South America

total dry land area — arable — pasture

This map from 1989 shows the main crops grown in each region, together with the most important type of livestock that is raised there — reindeer, cattle, sheep, or pigs.

The large pie chart shows the population of the world's regions. The small pie charts show how much of the total dry land in each region is used for crop growing and how much is pasture land. Overall, only 11 percent of the world's dry land area is used for cultivation.

Left *These people are plowing the soil by hand in the Katmandu Valley, Nepal.*

Below *Combine harvesters roll across huge wheat fields on the prairies of Montana.*

cleared for planting can be used only for around three years, by which time the fertility of the soil will be exhausted. The nutrient-rich layer is thin and is easily depleted. So the forest must be left to grow back over the land and revive the soil. All over the world, farmers know that they must either allow nature to replenish the soil or add some kind of fertilizer to replace the nutrients removed through crop cultivation.

Crops for food

Throughout history people have used as many as 3,000 plant species for food, although only around 150 have been grown commercially — to produce food to be sold. The need to grow more food for bigger populations has led farmers all over the world to concentrate on fewer and fewer species, and today most people in the world are fed on less than 20 major food crops. Four of these — wheat, rice, potatoes, and corn — now account for more than all other food crops combined.

Some regions, such as Latin America, just manage to meet their food needs. Others are unable to grow enough. For example, Africa has to feed 11 percent of the world's population on less than seven percent of the planet's total crop production. The com-bination of crops such as cassava and sorghum, which have little nutritional value, and regular periods of drought help to make Africa the region with the greatest number of hungry people in the world.

North America, Japan, Australia, and Western Europe all produce far more food than

Some countries, including many of those in Western Europe, produce more food than they need. These French apples have been left to rot.

in some Asian countries there is not enough to go around.

Overall, far less food is grown per person in the developing countries than in the developed countries, where more food is grown on less land mainly by using artificial fertilizers and pesticides. On average developed countries now use twice as much fertilizer as developing nations, who frequently cannot afford to import fertilizer.

Livestock farming

At the same time that people began to cultivate crops they also domesticated the wild ancestors of today's grazing animals and poultry. In some places keeping livestock for meat and milk became vital, especially in dry and semidesert areas where animals eat plants that humans cannot use. Livestock also provide fibers for clothing such as wool, camel hair, and leather, and lamp oil. Dung is also a very useful source of fertilizer or fuel.

Meat consumption varies widely around the world. Although the developing countries may possess more than 50 percent of the world's livestock, they consume less than 20 percent of the world's meat and milk. Meat consumption in developed countries costs the developing world in other ways: while children die of hunger in Africa, at least 40 percent of the world's edible grain supply is fed to livestock in Europe, Russia and the Other Independent Nations, and North America.

they need. Yet these areas all import a great deal of food to provide a more varied, though not necessarily healthier, diet. In general they feed their surplus grain production to livestock.

Asia has high rates of food production, but there is also a huge population to be fed, so

Other human foods, such as soybeans, are also used in animals feeds.

The United Nations estimates that on a vegetarian diet the world could support a population about six times greater than the present 5.2 billion. Just ten acres planted with soybeans can provide enough protein to feed 61 people for a lifetime; the same land used for beef production can feed two people.

Fishing

Seafood makes up less than five percent of the global diet, but it is an important source of protein, particularly in developing countries. In 1951 the global fish harvest was 21 million tons. The oceans were thought to be an unlimited resource, and fish catches rose by around seven percent each year until the mid-1970s. However, since 1975 catches

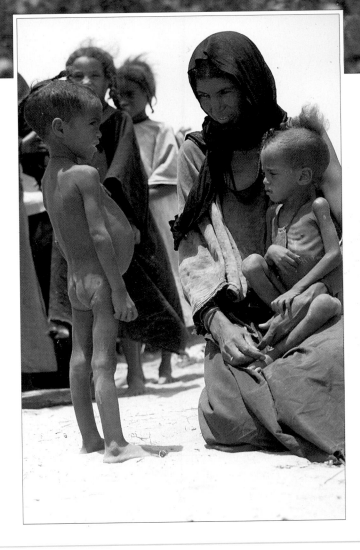

Right *These people are starving because a severe drought has killed their crops.*

take more than two-thirds of the catch off the coast of West Africa.

Industrialized farming

During the 1940s scientists began producing new seeds for farmers in the developed countries. These high-yielding seeds replaced lower-yielding traditional varieties. To make the most of the new seeds, large areas of land were drained and brought under cultivation for the first time. Many smaller fields were also combined to create larger fields more suited to mechanized farming.

The secret of the new seeds really lay in the way that they responded to irrigation, extra fertilizer, and pesticides. At first, yields increased dramatically, doubling within the first ten years. After that, farmers found they had to keep increasing the amount of chemicals they used to maintain the higher yields.

Left *A plane sprays pesticide on a crop grown as forage for livestock. The use of such chemicals has increased dramatically during the last 30 years.*

Below *The world's fish catch in 1986. Of the 35.7 million tons caught by ships from Asian countries, Japan accounted for 11 million tons.*

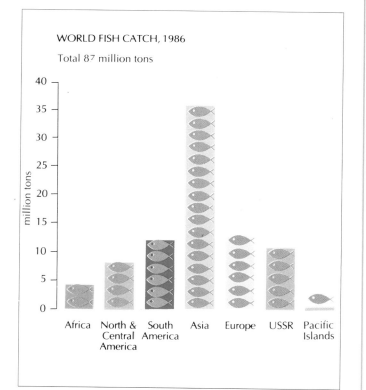

WORLD FISH CATCH, 1986

Total 87 million tons

have fallen slowly, reaching 87 million tons in 1986.

The combination of pollution in coastal waters and overfishing has led fisherman to go farther, use finer nets, and catch younger fish in order to stay in business. In doing so they know that fish stocks will continue to decline.

We have already overfished some species of whales and dolphins to the point of extinction or near extinction, and we are also taking far too many other fish from the northern oceans. For instance, North Atlantic halibut, cod, and haddock stocks have been reduced by 90 percent, and herring by at least 40 percent.

Nine developed countries now catch and sell one-third of the global catch for use in livestock feeds and fertilizers. What is more, having run down their own fisheries, they now send fleets to exploit those of other nations. For example, fishing fleets from Russia, Spain, Poland, France, and Japan now

Between 1961 and 1980 the developed nations doubled the amount of fertilizer they used; over the same period crop yields stayed more or less the same. Furthermore, the use of so many chemicals has created a range of problems for the environment. For example, around 70 percent of our water supplies are now used for irrigation; this can only be achieved by taking water from underground sources faster than natural processes can replace it. In some countries much of the fertilizer used over the past 40 years is polluting groundwater supplies. Even if the use of artificial fertilizers stopped today it would take many decades of rain to wash away their residue.

The use of pesticides has followed a similar pattern to that of fertilizers. At first they were seen as a miraculous tool. Later, pests began to develop resistance to the pesticides. It also became clear that the chemicals stayed in the environment far longer than was originally thought, killed wildlife, and polluted water supplies.

Some farmers believe they have no choice but to find an alternative way to grow food that uses fewer chemicals, creates less pollution, and uses animals to restore soil fertility. This approach is now known as organic farming. Other, more technological methods are being developed to increase food pro-

duction without harming the environment. Scientists are now attempting to use genetic engineering to develop crops that are resistant to pests and drought, need less water, and make better use of soil fertility. Moreover, in some cases they are looking back at local strains that have been grown in the past and that show high resistance.

The Green Revolution

After new seed varieties had been used successfully to increase agricultural yields in many developed countries, the same technology was exported to developing nations during the 1960s. This process was nicknamed the "Green Revolution" and its main aims were to increase food production, reduce hunger, and boost foreign trade.

Sure enough, in many areas high-yielding seed varieties increased production fourfold within ten years. However, from environmental, economic, and social viewpoints the Green Revolution proved to be a very mixed blessing. Each new irrigation plan required the construction of a dam. Villages upstream of such a dam were often com-

The countries shown as being "extremely dependent" on fertilizers each use more than 825 pounds per acre on their arable fields every year.

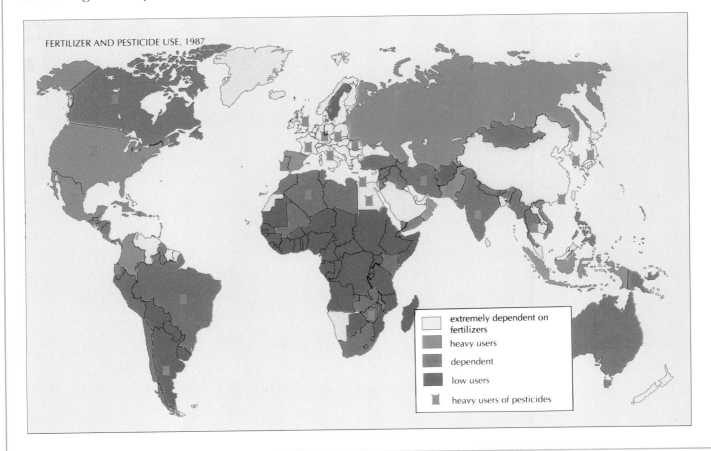

FERTILIZER AND PESTICIDE USE, 1987

extremely dependent on fertilizers

heavy users

dependent

low users

heavy users of pesticides

Above *This Japanese aid worker is helping farmers in Zambia to improve the way they grow food. The best form of aid is that which allows local people to help themselves.*

Right *One of the serious drawbacks to using large amounts of pesticides is that they can cause poisons to spread through the food chain. This black-headed gull has died as a result of taking in DDT, a highly toxic pesticide.*

pletely destroyed and the people in them forced to move. In some places, irrigation has also led to an increase in the salinity, or salt content, of the soil. When this occurs, there are several results. Soil fertility is reduced dramatically, crop yields fall, and soil erosion increases rapidly.

As in the developed world, it soon became clear that to keep their yields high farmers had to use more chemicals every year. However, many small farmers simply could not afford to buy ever-increasing quantities of expensive, imported seeds, fertilizers, and pesticides. A large number of farmers got into debt, and their only means of survival was to sell their land to their richer neighbors and migrate to the cities to join the urban poor.

DESERTIFICATION

Deserts occur naturally all over the world. The word "desert" literally means a "place that is deserted," although about 260 million people live in deserts or around their edges. We tend to associate deserts with very hot, very dry lands, covered with shifting sand dunes. A few deserts are like this, but most are made up of rock. Some, for example the Gobi Desert in central Asia, are actually very cold during the winter months, and even hot deserts are cold at night because there are no clouds to trap the heat of the day.
Deserts cover over 12 percent of the earth's land surface. Most occur around the tropics, where the winds have passed over thousands of miles of land, or over high mountain ranges, losing all their moisture. Areas receiving less than 10 inches of rainfall per year are classed as deserts. Many areas receive far less; in some rain may not fall for many years.

Right *More than 12 percent of the world's land is desert. The areas most at risk of desertification are on the edges of these natural deserts.*

The small graphs show how the temperature and rainfall varies throughout the year in three desert areas.

Top right *The Sahara Desert in Algeria. Not all deserts are hot and sandy like this part of the Sahara. Some, especially those at high altitudes, are very cold. Large areas of the Sahara and other deserts consist of rocks rather than sand dunes.*

ARCTIC OCEAN

GREENLAND
(Den)

ICELAND

IRELAND
UNITED
KINGDOM
NETH
BEL
W GER
POLAND
CZECH
HUNG
ROM
YUGOSLAVIA
BULG
ALB
GREECE
TURKEY

NORWAY
SWEDEN
FINLAND
DENMARK

UNION OF SOVIET SOCIALIST REPUBLICS

Ulaanbaatar
MONGOLIA

N KOREA
JAPAN
S KOREA

PACIFIC
OCEAN

FRANCE

SPAIN
PORTUGAL

ITALY

CYPRUS
LEBANON
ISRAEL
SYRIA
Mosul
IRAQ
JOR

AFGHANISTAN

CHINA

TAIWAN

HONG KONG

MOROCCO
TUNISIA

KUWAIT
BAHRAIN
QATAR
UAE

BHUTAN
B
DESH

ALGERIA
LIBYA
EGYPT
Aswan

SAUDI ARABIA

OMAN

INDIA

MYANMAR

WESTERN SAHARA

VERDE
MAURITANIA

MALI
NIGER
CHAD
SUDAN

YEMEN
AR
YEMEN PDR

DJIBOUTI

LAOS
THAILAND

SENEGAL
GAMBIA
GINEA-BISSAU
GUINEA
BURKINA
FASO
GHANA
NIGERIA

CAM
VIETNAM

PHILIPPINES

SIERRA LEONE
LIBERIA

IVORY
COAST

ETHIOPIA
SOMALIA

SRI LANKA

BRUNEI

TOGO
CAMEROON
EQUATORIAL GUINEA

KENYA

MALAYSIA
SINGAPORE

SAO TOME & PRINCIPE
GABON
CONGO
ZAIRE
R
TANZANIA

INDIAN
OCEAN

INDONESIA

PAPUA
NEW
GUINEA
SOLOMON
ISLANDS

COMOROS

ANGOLA
ZAMBIA
MALAWI

MADAGASCAR
MAURITIUS

ZIMBABWE
MOZAMBIQUE

AUSTRALIA

NAMIBIA
BOTSWANA

SOUTH
AFRICA

AREAS AT RISK OF
DESERTIFICATION
late 1980s

- very high risk
- high risk
- moderate risk
- existing desert
- other land
- severe land erosion

NEW
ZEALAND

41

Deserts on the move

Deserts are spreading, not naturally but as a result of the way land is treated by people. The areas most affected are those regions around true deserts, known as arid and semi-arid land. These areas receive between 10 and 23 inches of rainfall per year, although most falls at one time of year. In some years the rain fails completely. Although fertile, the soil is easily exhausted by too much cultivation or damaged when too many livestock — cattle, sheep, and goats — are grazed on it.

Much of this land is made up of open woodland and scrub, as well as grassland. Collecting wood for fuel and overgrazing by goats now threaten much of that woodland. When too many trees are lost, the exposed soil is easily eroded — washed or blown away — and so nothing can grow. This process, known as desertification, affects vast areas of land. It threatens millions of people with loss of their land, malnutrition, and often starvation.

The causes of desertification

The spread of deserts is not caused by drought or even overpopulation, although both make it worse. The main cause is the management, or mismanagement, of land. Many different factors lead to desertification, but it is important to understand that they are often interrelated and always far from simple.

Although it is often fertile, arid and semi-arid land land contains little organic material, or humus. In the past, farmers allowed land to remain uncultivated, or fallow, for a period to allow it to regenerate. Alternatively, they would cooperate with nomadic herders whose herd grazed the land for a time. Dung from the cattle and sheep fertilized the soil, and meat could be exchanged for the farmers' cereals.

In recent years increases in population and changes in traditional ways of life have put an end to such practices. In Niger, for example, the amount of grain harvested per acre has decreased steadily over the last 50 years due to overcultivation and an increase in the production of cash crops. In the U.S. in the 1920s, the traditional dry grazing lands of Texas, Kansas, and Oklahoma were plowed up to grow more profitable wheat. But good

Losing Ground

• One-third of the earth's land surface is arid or semiarid, supporting perhaps 600 million people. More than half this area is under direct threat of desertification.

• Every year 111 million acres of land are affected by desertification and 15 to 25 million acres completely lost to desert.

• It has been estimated that over 50 percent of India's land is now suffering from varying degrees of soil erosion.

• The Sahel, a region to the south of the Sahara Desert In Africa, suffers the worst wind erosion of soil in the world.

• Soil erosion and desertification are not confined to the poorer regions of the world, although they are hardest hit by its effects. A larger area of land is affected in the U.S., Canada, and Mexico than on the entire African continent.

• Virtually the entire agricultural region of Australia is threatened by poor stock-raising techniques.

• In Asia at least 40 percent of all land is at high risk of desertification; much of this is in arid areas of Russia and the Other Independent Nations.

• The cost of halting desertification worldwide is estimated at $2.5 billion a year. The loss of output from the productive land that is lost to deserts each year is estimated at ten times this figure.

cultivation methods were ignored, and by the early 1930s the soil was exhausted and damaged by constant plowing. Following two years of drought, a great storm in 1934 blew away 350 million tons of ruined soil, and much of the American Midwest became a desert. Although the U.S. now has a national Soil Conservation Service, it is estimated that 40 percent of American farms are still losing soil. These could benefit from techniques to avoid over-cultivation.

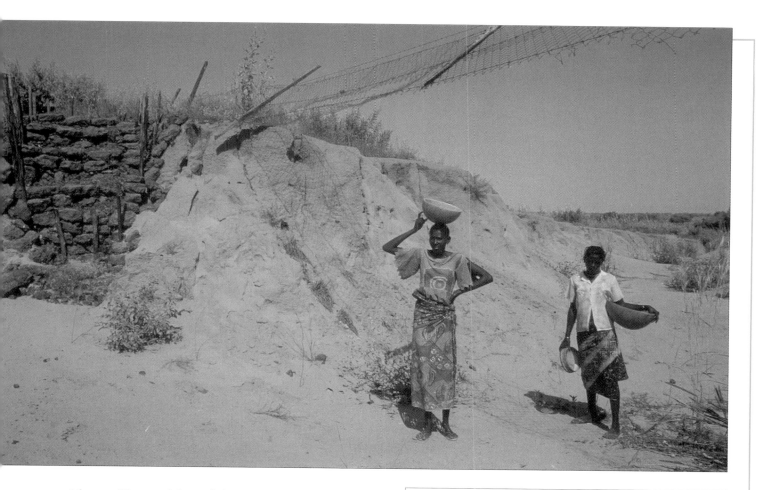

Above *The position of the fence in this picture shows where the level of the land used to be. Severe soil erosion has worn away more than nine feet of soil.*

Right *This diagram shows who gets what percentage of the money spent on a jar of coffee.*

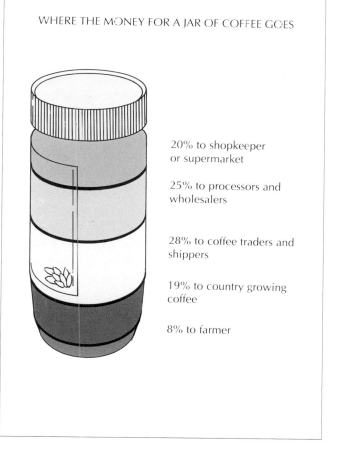

WHERE THE MONEY FOR A JAR OF COFFEE GOES

20% to shopkeeper or supermarket

25% to processors and wholesalers

28% to coffee traders and shippers

19% to country growing coffee

8% to farmer

All countries need exports to pay for goods they buy from other countries. They may earn money by growing cash crops, like tea, cotton, or coffee, which other (usually richer) countries cannot or will not grow themselves. The problem is that cash crops are often grown at the expense of the food crops that would feed local people. During the famines in the Sahel in the 1970s, exports of peanuts increased while local people died of starvation. In Mexico, 80 percent of children in rural areas are undernourished, while livestock — mainly cattle for export to North America — eat more grain than the entire human population of the country.

Cash crops are often grown on the best land, forcing small farmers to work for the cash crop companies, or to farm poorer land. The cash crops are often unsuitable for the land, requiring constant treatment with expensive chemicals that damage the soil. Meanwhile the poorer land, now supporting greater numbers of people, turns to desert.

In dry areas the land is often more suitable for grazing animals on the sparse natural vegetation than for growing crops.

In the past, people keeping livestock herds were nomadic, moving frequently and spreading their herds widely, preserving the grazing or rangelands. With increases in population and herd size, traditional grazing land is plowed up for cultivation and the remaining rangeland soon becomes overgrazed and damaged further by trampling. The old migration routes of the nomads are also disturbed and the traditional cooperation between the managers of the herd and the farmers breaks down.

In Senegal deep wells were bored to provide water for people and their livestock. The wells attracted nomadic herders who no longer needed to move their cattle. Soon the land was overgrazed and the soil badly damaged for miles around the wells. Simple solutions for African problems have often proved to create new problems. In the U.S. more than half the rangelands owned by private farmers are overgrazed. Soil erosion has cut in half the possible grass production.

Nearly 90 percent of people in poorer countries depend on wood as a building material and as a source of fuel. Much of this is collected locally from fallen branches or brushwood, but when this supply is gone trees are felled, and the dry woodlands begin to disappear. Demand from the growing cities is also immense, and vast amounts of wood and charcoal are illegally trucked into towns and sold to those who can afford it. And, as populations increase, more and more woodland is cleared for agriculture, including cash crops.

Trees slow down heavy rain before it reaches the soil; their roots stabilize the soil, particularly on hillsides; and their falling leaves add to its fertility. Trees literally hold back deserts. Loss of forests in tropical countries such as Brazil and Malaysia creates desertlike soil conditions even though these are not arid areas.

According to United Nations estimates, more than 100 million people worldwide experience acute shortages of fuelwood. Women in Burkina Faso may have to walk for four to six hours several times a week to gather enough firewood to cook a meal.

Overgrazing livestock on poor land is one of the main causes of desertification. This picture shows cattle in Nigeria.

It may seem surprising that the irrigation of land, by digging wells or channeling water from elsewhere, can lead to desertification. But if irrigated land is not well drained, the land rapidly becomes waterlogged and the salts in the irrigation water build up, making the land useless for growing crops. Irrigation water may also draw up deeper groundwater with a high salt content. On the Indus plain of Pakistan, 965 square miles of farmland is now salt desert as a result of poor irrigation programs. Too many wells may also have the effect of lowering the water table so that, eventually, all the wells become dry. Furthermore, irrigation projects can be as harmful as helpful, as in the case of the nomadic herders and the deep wells in Senegal.

So there are many complicated factors involved in the spread of deserts. Sometimes there is war within or between the countries involved, making life difficult for farmers and distribution of food impossible. Many of the poorer countries owe huge debts to the richer nations and have little money for their own development. Even if these debts are "written off," the countries

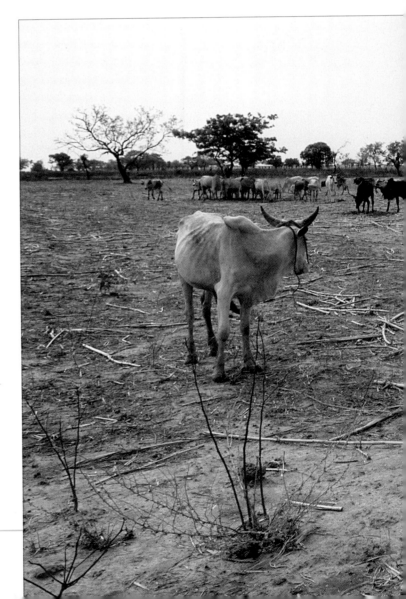

are still tied by the need to sell cash crops, often at very low prices, or to accept aid projects that may benefit the donor country more than the recipient.

Drought is a factor in the spread of deserts, and so is increasing population. But just as people can help to cause desertification, they can also be a factor, perhaps the major factor, in preventing it and turning back the spread of deserts.

This boy in Rwanda is collecting wood to be used as fuel.

Stopping the spread of deserts

There are many ways in which land can be managed in order to reduce the effects of soil erosion by wind and rain. The methods used will depend on the particular situation, the local conditions, and the materials available. They will only be successful when they are part of properly planned improvement programs that involve the communities who will benefit from their success and tackle the causes of desertification.

Cultivation methods can be improved so that more crops can be produced without damaging the soil. Drought-resistant crop varieties, like millet and sorghum, are already grown widely in arid countries. New crops such as grain amaranth and the lima bean have also been shown to be very resistant to drought. With an increase in the variety of crops grown, there is less likelihood of a total crop failure.

Higher production means that farmers are able to return to more traditional methods, such as crop rotation. A common four-year rotation is millet, cowpeas, peanuts, and a year of lying fallow.

Cowpeas provide fodder for cattle and also enrich the soil with nitrogen. Well-managed, usually small-scale, irrigation programs can improve crop yields dramatically and can be used to establish small vegetable and fruit farms to improve the nutrition of local people.

The problems of overgrazing are perhaps more difficult to solve. In the past, the great grasslands of the world were grazed by wild herds, such as bison in North America and saiga in Russia. These were hunted almost to extinction and domestic animals, often unsuited to the conditions, took their place. Better disease control and research into hardier animals that are more like the original inhabitants of the grasslands will improve meat production but may also lead to greater soil damage.

Tackling the problem of overgrazing does not necessarily mean a return to the "old ways," but a combination of traditional methods and new techniques such as better breeding, disease control, and better distribution. On the southern edges of the Koroli desert in Kenya, the Redille tribe lived in moveable camps, following their herds of sheep, goats, and camels as they searched for the best grass. An attempt was made to settle the tribe in villages around deep wells, but after several years of drought much of the tribe's livestock died. Now the Kenyan government is attempting to bring the Redille tribe back to a somewhat nomadic way of life by providing many small wells throughout the region and supplying other benefits and services associated with a more settled way of life.

Stopping the loss of trees is perhaps the single most important act that would halt, and even turn back, the spread of deserts. There are trees that can complement crop or livestock production. The acacia is an example: it fertilizes the soil by adding nitrogen and phosphorus, its pods make nutritious animal feed, and crops such as millet can be grown underneath it. Later the wood can be used as a building material and for fuel.

Planting trees can cut down on soil erosion by wind and rain. These plantings are called shelterbelts. In Rajasthan, India, 930 miles have been planted, using trees that be harvested for fodder and fuelwood. In one region of Niger, Africa, a windbreak program has increased cereal production by 15 percent, while in another region there are plans to produce 50,000 acacia, eucalyptus, and orange seedlings a year to stabilize sand dunes and help restore agricultural land as a first step toward proper forest regeneration.

More efficient wood-burning stoves will reduce the amount of fuelwood that is required for cooking. If these can be locally and cheaply manufactured, like the United

These are some of the ways in which desertification can be halted. Not all would be used in the same place.

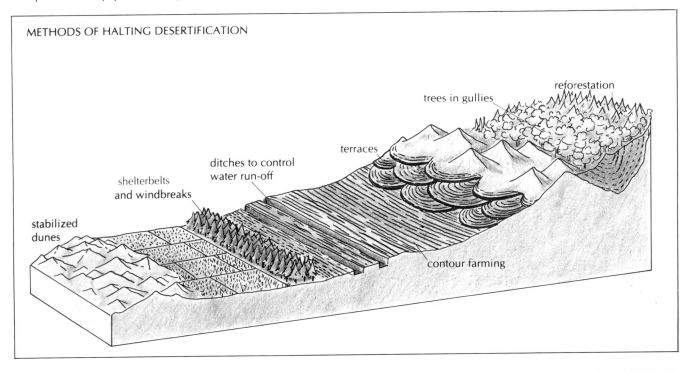

METHODS OF HALTING DESERTIFICATION

reforestation

trees in gullies

terraces

ditches to control water run-off

shelterbelts and windbreaks

stabilized dunes

contour farming

villages in this region of India.

In 1972 a small Oxfam experiment in Yatenga, Burkina Faso, began with the building of low, U-shaped earth walls to catch rainwater for tree seedlings planted inside them. The local people adapted the technique to help grow food crops, constructing low barriers of stones, stalks, and branches across their fields to halt water runoff. Now the stone lines, or *diguettes*, have been built on over 12,000 acres. A simple but effective technique has been devised to measure contours on the almost flat land so the *diguettes* can be sited correctly. Now a constant stream of visitors come to learn how this simple technique is done.

Both these examples may seem tiny compared to the areas affected by desertification worldwide. But they show what can be done when people understand the problem and are given the tools to tackle it. Similar

Above *These plants are being grown to stabilize the sand dunes at the edge of the Sahara in Tunisia.*

Right *This desert area has been reclaimed. Crops can now be grown here in the shelter of the windbreaks around the field.*

Nations Environment Program's "Jiko" stove, success is more likely.

Two success stories

In the Indian state of Gujarat a number of villages established plantations on communal grazing lands. Mixtures of seedlings for timber, fuelwood, and fodder were supplied by the forestry department, which worked closely with village councils. The villagers protected the plantations from grazing and fuelwood thieves and, in return, shared in the profits when the trees were harvested. The program has been copied in 3,500

examples, both large and small, of local people successfully applying a technique, can be found throughout the world.

So desertification has little to do with droughts, too many people, or bad luck. It has a lot to do with poverty, the relationship between the richer and poorer nations, and the way we all manage and use land. All? Yes, because many of our own decisions — what we buy, how much we are prepared to pay for it, even whether we bother to stick to the footpath rather than take the worn shortcut across the grass — affect the spread of deserts.

ENERGY CRISIS

The world uses vast amounts of energy every year. Because we use it in many different forms — coal, gas, oil, electricity, wood, and so on — we need a single yardstick to measure how much we are really using; this is the mtoe, or million tons of oil equivalent. It tells us how much energy we would use in a certain situation if it were in the form of oil.

We consume just over 9,000 mtoe each year, 78 percent of it from fossil fuels. Oil itself provides about 34 percent, coal about 25 percent and natural gas about 19 percent. The rest is made up of about 5 percent from nuclear-generated electricity, 6 percent from hydroelectricity (water power), and 11 percent from fuel from living things, and other sources such as solar, wind, and geothermal power.

Right *This map from 1989 shows the major reserves of fossil fuels. The small graphs illustrate the estimated size of the coal, oil, and gas reserves in each region and the number of years they will last. The arrows show the movements of oil and gas around the world, from the areas that produce them to those where they are used. The thicker the arrow, the greater the amount of fuel moved.*

Top right *Energy use in the various regions of the world in 1989*

48

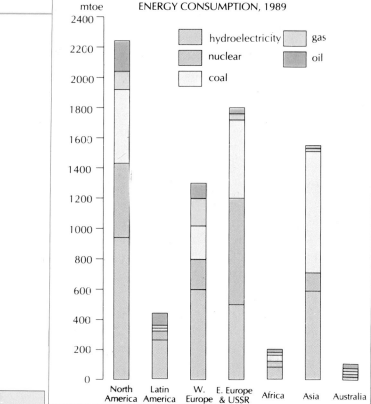

ENERGY CONSUMPTION, 1989

mtoe

hydroelectricity   gas

nuclear   oil

coal

North America   Latin America   W. Europe   E. Europe & USSR   Africa   Asia   Australia

Who is using the energy?

The diagram (left) shows the energy consumption, in 1989, of the seven regions of the world, in the different sources of energy. Notice that the only figures used are those for commercial fuels — wood and animal waste, for example, are not included — so the total for the developing countries, mainly in Africa, Latin America, and most of Asia, is misleading.

Four regions — North America, Eastern Europe and the U.S.S.R., Western Europe, and Asia — took by far the bigger share. In Asia the developed countries of Japan, South Korea, and Taiwan accounted for over 33 percent of the total, and China took most of the rest. Clearly the parts of the world that are industrialized, developed countries use

Left *Like most other manu-facturing processes, making synthetic fibers, such as nylon, uses a lot of energy. The raw materials used to produce many such fibers are made from oil.*

Below *Farmers in developed countries use more machin-ery and therefore consume more energy than those in developing nations.*

more energy than the developing countries.

One of the reasons for this is that, in the developed world, most people are em-ployed in industry, including manufacturing and service industries — in factories, stores, and offices. Large amounts of energy are consumed in manufacturing processes and in heating and lighting factories and office buildings. Developing countries have much less industry, and so they consume much less energy in these ways.

Another reason why developed countries consume more energy than those in the developing world has to do with food. Al-though most people in developing countries work in agriculture, in the developed world agriculture consumes more energy. This is because farmers in developed countries use much more intensive methods — more ma-chinery, artificial fertilizers, and pesticides, which require energy both to make and to use. After leaving the farm the food is trans-ported farther and more energy is spent on processing it.

The third reason is transportation. In the developed world there are many more com-mercial and privately owned vehicles. In the U.S. there are about 750 road vehicles per thousand people. In contrast, the figures for India and Indonesia are 2 and 15. It is a similar picture for air and rail transportation. However, one form of transportation used much more in developing countries is the bicycle. In 1987 more people bought bikes in China than bought cars in the whole world. China now has about 500 million bikes, and India 45 million.

The fourth major way in which people in the developed world use more energy is in heating their homes. This is partly because they are often in cooler climates and partly because they can afford a much higher degree of comfort. Although, on the whole, Americans are more aware of wasteful heating practices, there is still room for improvement. Generally, homes and offices are kept at lower temperatures. People are more energy conscious now. They are especially careful not to heat unused rooms. Also

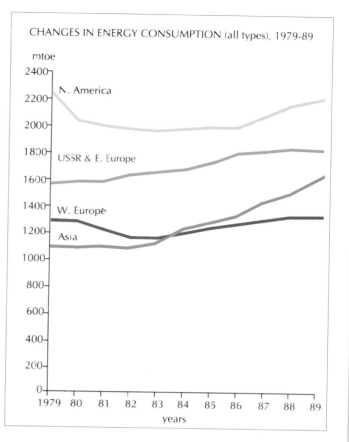

CHANGES IN ENERGY CONSUMPTION (all types), 1979-89

Above *Between 1979 and 1989, the change in the amount of energy used varied from region to region. This was partly due to the ways regions reacted to the sudden oil-price rise in 1978 – 1979.*

many homes are evaluated in terms of testing for heat loss, proper insulation, and construction.

Patterns of consumption

The diagram above shows how the consumption of energy in the four main regions changed between 1979 and 1989. The world price of oil rose sharply in 1978 – 79, and this led to an economic slowdown in many countries. In North America and Western Europe there were several years in which energy consumption did not increase, and between 1979 and 1989 there was only a small rise overall. Yet Eastern Europe and the U.S.S.R. and Asia increased their consumption significantly.

In part this is because Asia (except for Japan) and Eastern Europe and the U.S.S.R. were much less able than Canada, the U.S., and Western Europe to introduce energy-saving methods and equipment. It may not seem fair that the poorer countries were less able to change things to spend less on energy, but it is true.

51

Another reason is that the Soviet-led communist systems that were then present in Eastern Europe and the U.S.S.R. fixed the price of energy way below the world price. So there was less reason to change the old, inefficient ways of using energy.

China — which uses over 40 percent of Asia's energy — also has a communist system that kept the price of energy low so that efficiency did not improve much. Asia also had a much bigger rise in population (as did Africa and Latin America) than the developed world, which pushed up energy use. A further reason for Asia's rise in energy consumption between 1979 and 1989 was that Japan did much better economically than the rest of the world. This meant that it could afford both to find ways of using energy more efficiently and to use more energy altogether.

Reserves

Reserves of fossil fuels are constantly going up; not the real, actual fuel under the ground, but the "proved reserves." This term means the portion of the total actual reserves that we are reasonably certain we can extract from known places with today's technology and at today's prices. So, proved reserves go up if technology improves, enabling more to be extracted, and if the price goes up, making it more profitable to extract them from deep underground, sand, shale, or offshore seabeds. New discoveries also add to proved reserves.

There is still the problem that fossil fuels will run out eventually. Finding new reserves, like the oil and gas fields in the North Sea and Alaska, becomes more difficult all the time. But there are two other important problems.

First, much of the world's fossil fuel reserves are in extremely inconvenient places. The Middle East, for example, has seen many wars in recent years, often with interference from outside the region, and these events can disrupt the extraction and movement of oil. Russia and the Other Independent Nations, which still produce 20 percent of the world's oil, also have many serious problems — economic crises, a political crises, and a nationality crises. The breakup of the Soviet empire may have an unpredictable effect on the world's supply of oil.

The other major problem is not with future supply, but with possible future demand. One-quarter of the world's population now accounts for 70 percent of fossil fuel use. If the developing world were to start using fossil fuels at the rate of the developed world, the length of time that proved reserves are expected to last would be cut by 65 percent. This change might be a "fair" one, but it would be a disaster for energy supply.

However, damage to the unburned fossil fuels supply may be less threatening than damage from burned fossil fuels, that is called pollution.

Pollution

The main pollutants from burning fossil fuels are carbon monoxide, carbon dioxide, sulfur dioxide, nitrogen oxide, particulates (minute

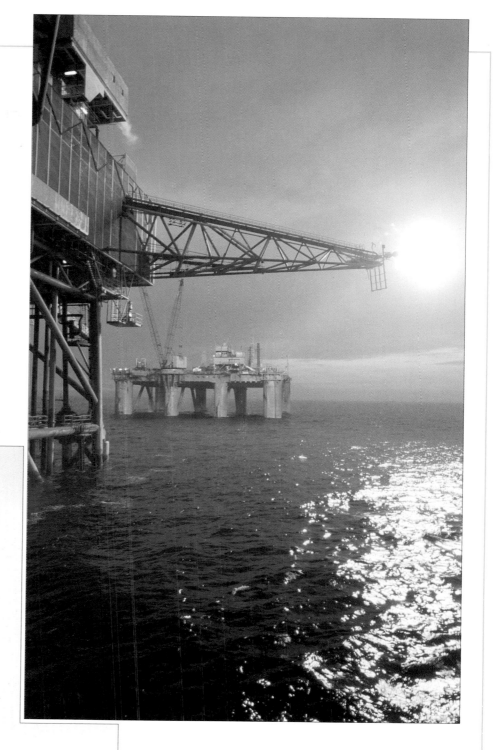

Right *An oil production platform in the North Sea. It is increasingly difficult to find major new reserves of oil because almost all of the most promising areas have already been explored.*

Below *Pollution produced by burning fossil fuels can damage people's health and disturb the ecological balance of the planet.*

particles of unburned or partly burned fuels), and ozone. In most countries the gasoline contains lead, a dangerous pollutant that is no longer used as an additive in gasoline in the U.S.

Pollution from fossil fuels affects people's health, the trees and lakes, and the atmosphere of the whole globe. The health effects can be terrible. Carbon monoxide affects the ability of the blood to carry oxygen around the body. Sulfur dioxide and particulates cause lung disease, and lead attacks the nervous system. Ozone attacks the eyes and lungs. Pollution caused by fossil fuels is discussed in other chapters. For example, pages 58 – 60 explain the causes and effects of acid rain, while pages 75 – 78 cover the threat of global warming.

The alternatives

If we are to cut down on the amount of fossil fuels burned and reduce the level of pollution they cause, we must find other forms of energy to use. There are several possible alternatives.

Nuclear power: Although it costs a lot of energy to build a nuclear power plant, once built it saves a great deal of fossil fuel and therefore reduces pollution. Today's nuclear plants keep a billion tons of carbon dioxide out of the atmosphere each year. There are also benefits in terms of reduced acid rain. Another benefit is that fewer people have been killed while working to produce nuclear power than in coal mining.

However, the arguments against nuclear power have been getting stronger. Two major accidents — at Three Mile Island in Pennsylvania in 1979 and at Chernobyl in the U.S.S.R. in 1986 — have made many people very concerned about safety. Disposing of the dangerous waste products from nuclear power is still an unsolved problem.

The shattered nuclear reactor at Chernobyl, after an explosion in 1986

The radiation released from nuclear power plants into the air, soil, and water is a great potential health hazard. Moreover, the costs of building and running nuclear power plants — and closing them down when they become too old — are enormous.

Around the world, only 94 nuclear plants are currently being built — the lowest figure in 15 years. As old plants are shut down, the total number in use may even drop. Solving the fossil fuel problems by building nuclear plants would require making amazing savings on building costs, spending large sums of money on safety, and finding ways of disposing of the radioactive waste. Then, in order to make a big difference, many hundreds of nuclear plants would have to be built at the same time.

Renewable energy: Energy from renewable sources is presently being used instead of fossil fuels, keeping more than a billion tons of carbon dioxide out of the atmosphere. This is equal to the pollution savings with nuclear power, but renewable sources may be a better prospect in the long run because they are much cheaper to build and run, and they are clean — no pollution is

A windfarm in the U.S. Electricity is produced by the spinning blades of the aerogenerators.

which generates electricity directly from sunlight, and for solar power stations where solar rays are concentrated onto a hotspot to boil water and drive turbines that produce electricity.

Wind power: There are 20,000 windmills generating electricity worldwide, mainly in the U.S. and Denmark. Other European countries are also developing wind power programs and in the future may have windfarms out at sea.

Power from water: Many countries now have hydroelectric power stations, which use the energy of falling water to generate electricity. Tidal and wave power stations are also in operation. However, tidal power stations can have serious ecological effects, and wave power costs are uncertain.

caused when a solar panel or a windmill is in use, and there are no waste products.

Solar power: All around the world, even in countries far from the tropics, solar panels could heat water for millions of buildings. Passive solar design — making sure that buildings receive as much energy as possible direct from the sun — and good conservation measures could cut pollution generated by heating buildings by 75 percent.

In sunnier parts of the world, there are excellent prospects for photoelectric effect,

Although many countries produce some of the energy they need from renewable sources, only a tiny proportion of the world's energy is made in this way.

Geothermal energy: The rocks below the earth's surface are hot and can be used as a source of energy. In some places, such as Iceland, hot water rises from the rocks to the surface and is used to heat homes and factories. In other parts of the world, water is pumped down to the rocks to be heated and is brought back to the surface. If the water is hot enough, it can be used to generate electricity. There are now geothermal power stations in 18 countries.

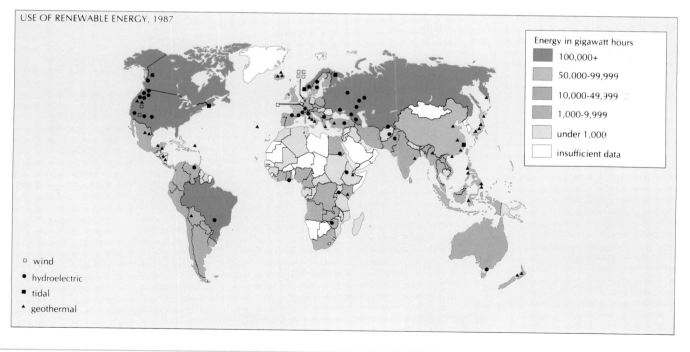

USE OF RENEWABLE ENERGY, 1987

Energy in gigawatt hours
- 100,000+
- 50,000-99,999
- 10,000-49,999
- 1,000-9,999
- under 1,000
- insufficient data

□ wind
● hydroelectric
■ tidal
▲ geothermal

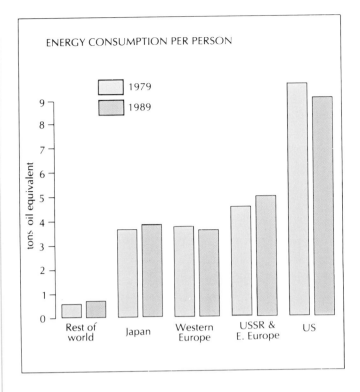

ENERGY CONSUMPTION PER PERSON

1979
1989

Most energy is used in the developed countries of the world.

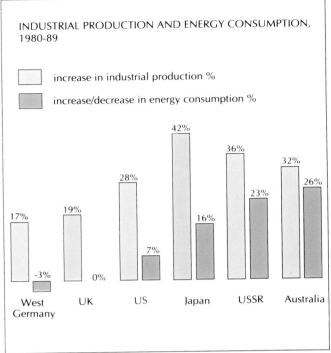

INDUSTRIAL PRODUCTION AND ENERGY CONSUMPTION, 1980-89

increase in industrial production %

increase/decrease in energy consumption %

A lot of the world's energy is used for industrial production.

Biomass: Growing our fuel could bring a double benefit. If we grow more wood than we burn, the production of carbon dioxide is cut both while the trees are growing and when they are burned instead of fossil fuel. Burning the methane gas given off from dumps and landfills is also useful because unburned methane is one of the gases that add to global warming. We could, of course, burn more of our garbage to provide heat, but clearly we could not both burn it and recycle it!

Using less energy
But the most important thing about all energy, whether or not it is renewable, is to use less of it.

We can use less energy in two main ways. One is by increasing efficiency —getting more light per kilowatt of power, or more miles per gallon of gas, for example. The other is conservation —devising methods of avoiding the need to use so much energy; for example, building houses that need less heating.

Since the big oil price increase of 1973, during the last Arab-Israeli war, the world has saved about $300 billion worth of energy. If the developed nations could save another three percent per year, they would be able to keep another 4 billion tons of

carbon out of the atmosphere by the year 2010.

The diagram above left shows how much energy is used per person in different regions of the world, and how this has changed since 1979. It is obvious where most of the energy is being used, and where and when the main improvements have come. The diagram above right takes into account the economies of the countries concerned. For each country there are two figures — the percentage increase in goods produced by that country's industries between 1980 and 1989, and the percentage increase in the country's energy consumption during the same period.

Efficiency: Different countries can have very different levels of efficiency in their use of energy in industry. One important way of increasing overall energy efficiency is to improve industrial methods. Not long ago, a ton of U.S. raw steel cost much more in energy to produce than a ton of Japanese raw steel. However, the U.S. is now improving its methods of steel production and reducing the amount of energy used. The U.S. energy consumption, per ton of raw steel produced, has improved by 40 percent since 1975.

Transportation: The world now has 500 million vehicles, producing a total of

550 million tons of carbon each year. There will almost certainly be a lot more cars in the year 2010, producing much more pollution. However, if cars can be produced that use fuel more efficiently than today's models, the amount of pollution could actually lessen considerably.

The best way to save fuel and cut pollution would be to use fewer cars. Buses and trains give about 14 times as many miles per person per gallon of fuel, even compared with an economical small car. Bicycles are far better still.

Lighting: This uses about 17 percent of our electricity. That figure can be cut easily by the use of new low-watt bulbs. They use far less energy and last longer. Refrigerators and other household appliances could be much more efficient. The tough standards for energy efficiency are a plus. Major appliances are evaluated for energy efficiency.

Electricity itself could be produced in a more efficient way in many places. A method known as District Heating or Combined

A traffic jam in Bangkok, Thailand. Cars and other vehicles use a lot of fuel and cause severe pollution problems.

Heat and Power is already in use in some places; it is a good example of greater efficiency at work. In a normal coal- or oil-fired power station, 70 percent of the heat from the fuel goes up the chimney into the air and is wasted. In a District Heating station, it is used to heat water for houses, factories, shopping centers, offices, and so on — doubling the energy obtained from each ton of fuel.

Heating: This is the form in which we use most of our energy, and it is an easy form to conserve. It is technologically very simple, and quite cheap, to build energy-conserving houses. In the U.S. building codes now require that certain grades of insulation, which work to keep heat in, be used at various places in the house. Increasing these minimum standards for insulation would be a good way to cut the amount of energy needed to heat a house. The homeowner would regain the cost of the extra insulation in money saved on fuel, and the environment would benefit.

We all have a choice to make: do we continue wasting energy, running down the world's fuel supplies and risking global warming, or do we change our ways?

AIR POLLUTION

A layer of gases, water vapor, and dust envelops the earth and supports life on it. It is called the atmosphere. Compared to the size of the earth, the layer is very thin: If the earth were the size of a football, the atmosphere would be the thickness of a piece of plastic-wrap around it.
As well as providing the air that plants and animals need to stay alive, the atmosphere distributes moisture around the earth, prevents too much harmful solar radiation from reaching the surface, and regulates temperature. However, by releasing smoke, fumes, and other pollutants into the atmosphere, we risk damaging this protective, life-supporting layer.

Air pollution — a world problem

Air pollution is not only found in areas where there are lots of factories. Once in the air, pollutants can be carried by the wind for several days and travel hundreds of miles. The environment in countries producing very little pollution can be damaged by pollution carried in the wind from other countries. Canada, for example, complains that much of the damage to its lakes and forests is caused by air pollution from the U.S.

Burning fossil fuels for the energy they provide is the major cause of air pollution. The main pollutants are sulfur dioxide, nitrogen oxides, hydrocarbons, and particulates (that is, particles of soot, dirt, and unburned fossil fuels). The highly industrialized countries use most of the world's energy and are responsible for most of the air pollution. Of the 100 million tons of sulfur dioxide put into the atmosphere every year, the U.S. creates about 30 million tons.

So many countries are experiencing damage to their environment from air pollution that it has become a global problem requiring international solutions. International organizations, like the United Nations Environment Program, and regional organizations, such as the European Community, are trying to persuade countries to agree on stronger air pollution controls.

Acid rain

Air pollution is a major cause of acid rain. Fumes created when fossil fuels are burned are discharged into the atmosphere. Some fall to the ground quickly, but

In the past, acid rain affected mainly the countries of the developed world, but many developing countries are now beginning to suffer.

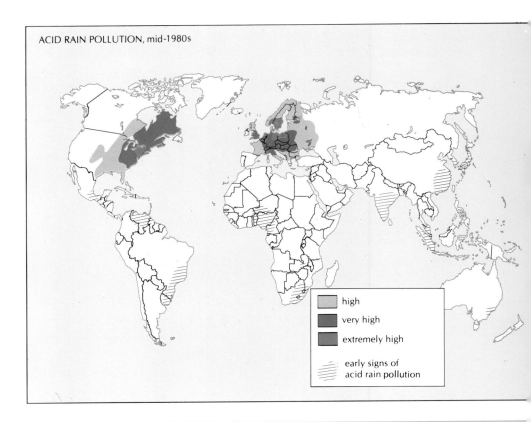

ACID RAIN POLLUTION, mid-1980s

high
very high
extremely high
early signs of acid rain pollution

others, especially those from tall smoke stacks, are absorbed by moisture in the air. As a result of chemical changes they become weak acids. Eventually, the moisture returns to the earth as acid rain, often hundreds of miles away from the source of the pollution. Although it is usually called acid rain, it might actually fall as snow, mist, or dew.

Acid rain can cause serious damage to the environment. If it falls where rocks and soils are alkaline, such as in chalk and limestone areas, the acid is neutralized and there is relatively little damage. If it falls where the rocks are acid, such as granite, the acid is not neutralized. Sulfur dioxide has damaged almost 75 percent of Europe's forests.

Large areas of Canada, Scandinavia, and Central Europe suffer a lot of dam-

Noise pollution is another by-product of our overcrowded roads.

age because they have acid rocks and are downwind from major industrial areas. However, acid rain is also becoming a problem in Venezuela, the east coast of Brazil, parts of West Africa, central India, eastern China, South Korea, Japan, Malaysia, Indonesia, and eastern Australia. In fact, wherever there is industry there are signs of environmental damage from acid rain.

Although many animals and plants, including decid-

A diver photographs the only life still flourishing in a Swedish lake affected by acid rain — the carpet of blue-green algae that covers the lake bed.

uous trees, are affected by acid rain, coniferous trees and wildlife in lakes and rivers suffer most. Damage to coniferous trees can be recognized by yellow spots on the needles, fewer needles, dead branches at the top of the tree, and badly developed root systems that allow the trees to blow over more easily. In Czechoslovakia 70 percent of the forests are damaged by acid rain, and in some areas hillsides that were once forested have become bare. Other parts of Eastern Europe have also been affected.

Many of the plants and animals that live in lakes and rivers cannot survive if the water becomes too acid. Acid rain washes poisonous heavy metals like aluminum out of the soil and into waterways where they harm living things. The number of fish and insects decreases until, in very acid lakes with a pH of around 4.5, there is little or no life. The acidity of things is measured in pH: pH7 is neutral, above 7 is alkaline, and below 7 is acid. Water with pH5 is ten times more acid than water with pH6 and 100 times more acid than that with pH7.

Buildings, too, can be damaged by acid rain. The rapid deterioration of the stonework on the Parthenon in Greece has been caused mainly by air pollution originating in the city of Athens. Other cities in Europe have struggled with damage to monuments caused by acid rain, too.

The long-term solution to acid rain is to reduce air pollution. This can be done, but it is costly and takes time. Sulfur dioxide is a major cause of acid rain. Power stations burning coal or oil are the main source. The amount of sulfur dioxide produced can be reduced by burning natural gas, which contains virtually no sulfur, burning coal or oil from sources that are naturally low in sulfur, or by removing the sulfur dioxide from the smoke before it reaches the atmosphere. Many countries have agreed to reduce the amount of sulfur dioxide they put into the atmosphere by 30 percent before the end of the century. Countries seriously affected by acid rain say that a reduction of 80 percent is needed.

In the short term there are some temporary solutions. Crushed limestone can be put into lakes or spread on the ground to help neutralize the acid rain. The main drawback is that areas need to be treated again after a few years, and the treatment is expensive.

A layer of photochemical smog hangs over a town on the U.S.-Mexican border. The smog is caused by the effects of sunlight on fossil fuel pollution.

Pollution from vehicles

By the year 2007, there should be no gas or diesel vehicles on the roads in Los Angeles. Only vehicles powered by electricity or cleaner fuels, such as ethanol, will be allowed. Air pollution in southern California is such a serious problem that drastic action is being taken. The authorities estimate that it will cost about $2.8 billion a year to make the changes, but this is small compared to the $13 billion cost of lower agricultural production and higher health bills resulting from air pollution.

Before 2007, other measures are likely to be introduced in southern California, including the outlawing of all free parking, enforcing car-pooling programs, and running all public and company vehicles on ethanol rather than gas or diesel. These actions are needed even though the area has the strongest vehicle exhaust emission controls in the world. Southern California is actively pursuing steps to control pollution.

Around the world there are over 500 million vehicles. Southern California, with 6 million, is not the only area facing terrible air pollution from vehicles, but it is one of the most active in trying to implement solutions. Motor vehicles are a major source of air pollution in an around most cities. Thousands of vehicles are concentrated in a small area, and the fumes enter the air at the same level as people are breathing and plants are growing. Between the cities,

POLLUTION CAUSED BY CARS mid-1980s

75%

48%

13%

3%

carbon monoxide

nitrogen oxides

dirt and dust

sulfur oxides

Above *This diagram shows the breakdown on the air pollution caused by cars.*

major roads pollute the air of the rural areas as well.

In hot, sunny weather there is an additional problem. The pollutants react with the strong sunlight to form ozone. During the hottest part of the day, levels of this poisonous gas frequently exceed maximum recommended levels in many major cities and in the countryside around them. In some countries the weather forecast warns people when pollution levels are going to be high, so that old people, children, and those with breathing or heart problems will stay inside and be protected from the ozone.

Cutting pollution

There are two ways to reduce the air pollution caused by motor vehicles. One is to reduce the amount of pollution coming from each vehicle, and the other is to reduce the use of motor vehicles.

Today's vehicles use less fuel and produce less pollution than those built as little as ten years ago because of improvements to the design of the engines. However, the amount of traffic is increasing so rapidly that the total amount of pollution is not dropping. To curb pollution, many governments are introducing much stricter controls. Europe is

Above *Some people wear masks to try to keep out the poisonous fumes of city traffic.*

moving to require all new cars to have catalytic converters by 1993. In the U.S. this requirement has been law for some years. A catalytic converter, fitted to the exhaust of the car, removes most of the carbon monoxide, nitrogen oxides, and hydrocarbons that cause pollution. However, it does not remove carbon dioxide, one of the major causes of global warming. The exhaust fumes from diesel engines, too, will have to be much cleaner.

Lead, which in some countries is added to gas to improve an engine's performance, ends up in the air along with the other pollutants. It is poisonous and very dangerous for young children. Oil companies have steadily reduced the amount of lead in leaded gas. Most cars on the road today in the U.S. use unleaded gas. Catalytic converters will only work on cars that use unleaded gas. At this time most European cars are still run on leaded gas.

Drivers can help reduce pollution by sometimes choosing to go by public transportation, buying smaller cars, and driving more smoothly and more slowly. Surveys have revealed that although people realize their vehicle is a major cause of pollution, they are unwilling to give it up, car pool, or drive more slowly!

Reducing pollution from individual vehicles is unlikely to reduce air pollution in the long term because more and more vehicles are being used. Improved public transportation would persuade some people to leave their cars at home, but regulations are needed to tackle the problem effectively. In Athens, Greece, for example, cars with even-number and odd-number license plates are allowed into the city center on alternate days.

Air quality in urban areas

Air pollution is worst in large cities where there are many buildings, factories, and vehicles in a small area. The pollutants enter the air in such quantities that they are not diluted to safe levels by the air. Much of the pollution comes from burning fossil fuels to provide the energy for heating buildings, powering vehicles and machines, generating electricity, and making things. But the air is polluted by many other chemicals as well, some of which are poisonous and very damaging if they become too concentrated in the air. The cloud of gas that escaped in 1984 when there was an accident at a factory in Bhopal, India, killed over 4,000 people living nearby. Another 20,000 people suffered injuries from this gas.

Some large cities in the U.S., especially Los Angeles, Chicago, and New York, have a higher rate of air pollution than most cities. When the air is particularly bad, conditions are aggravated by air pollution, and the occurrences of these diseases are much higher in industrial towns than in rural areas. However, air pollution in the cities of Eastern Europe and newly industrializing nations like China or Mexico is much worse. There are fewer controls because the equipment needed to reduce pollution is expensive. With poverty and unemployment the highest priorities, governments are reluctant to impose expensive controls on industry.

Action to reduce pollution

People and governments are now much more aware of the importance of clean air for all living things and the dangers of continuing to pollute the atmosphere. We need

Above *The chimney of a wood-pulp factory belches pollution into the air.*

Right *Demonstrators in Budapest, Hungary, protest air pollution. The countries of Eastern Europe have severe pollution problems.*

those with respiratory problems suffer. Laws have been passed at the Federal level, like the Clean Air Act of the 1970's, to improve the quality of the air. Regulations, including emissions standards, are now in place. Los Angeles has its own air pollution control district that issues a smog alert, to warn people about the danger. The air now looks much cleaner and the smogs are less of a problem than they were in the past. Most of the highly industrialized nations now have similar laws to try and keep the air in the cities clean.

Although most industrialized countries have pollution control laws, the problems still exists. Asthma, bronchitis, and heart

to use the earth's resources to improve our lives, but at the same time we must not damage the earth that provides these resources.

The problem has been recognized but there are no simple or cheap answers. Progress is being made in reducing air pollution. The leading industrial nations have agreed to reduce sulfur dioxide emissions from large industrial works and the major pollutants from vehicle exhausts. New pollution control technologies are being developed, and industry is being encouraged to use them according to the principle of using the "best available technology not entailing excessive costs."

POLLUTED WATERS

Almost every day rivers, lakes, seas, and oceans are being polluted. On television and in newspapers there are frequent reports of oil disasters, pollution by toxic chemicals, and damage caused by acid rain. In many places, untreated or partially treated sewage is being pumped into the sea, causing severe pollution. This is particularly true around the Mediterranean, and it has serious consequences for the tourist industry and the local population. All of these problems are threatening to damage one of our most precious resources — the water we all need to live — and to disturb the ecological balance of our planet.

Below *All over the world, rivers, lakes, and seas are being polluted with a wide range of domestic, industrial, and agricultural wastes.*

Out in the oceans, ships dump their waste oil and tanker accidents produce vast oil slicks that kill marine plants and animals.

POLLUTED RIVERS AND SEAS

- severe or persistent coastal pollution
- oil slicks
- deep sea dump sites
- severely polluted rivers

Our drinking water

The oceans cover about 70 percent of the surface of the earth and contain a vast quantity of salt water. Only three percent of the water on the earth's surface is fresh water. Fresh water is essential to life on earth. Plants, humans, and other animals depend on it for their survival.

Most of the world's fresh water can be found in the frozen polar ice caps and mountain glaciers. The air also contains fresh water, in the form of vapor, and the

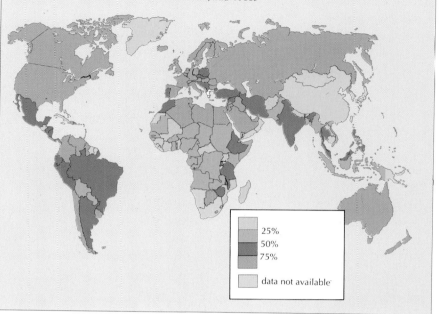

PEOPLE WHO HAVE SAFE DRINKING WATER, mid-1980s

25%
50%
75%
data not available

Above *In many developing countries, only a small proportion of the population has access to clean drinking water. In India, 97 percent of the available water is used in farming and industry.*

rest lies on or under the earth's surface — in lakes, rivers, and ponds or as groundwater in the rocks and soil beneath our feet.

Fresh water is essential to the drinking water supply, and as the world's population increases so does the demand for clean drinking water. Because of environmental pollution, it is increasingly difficult to maintain the supply of good drinking water. Illegal dumping of toxic chemicals can affect the water supply. The pumping of industrial waste into rivers means that many chemicals find their way into the environment and into reservoirs from which drinking-water supplies are taken. As a result, increasingly complicated equipment and techniques are required for purification.

The polluted Rhine

The Rhine River is sometimes called Europe's largest open sewer pipe because serious leakages and dumping of industrial and domestic waste are frequent occurrences. Tens of millions of people depend on the Rhine for drinking water. Following an explosion and fire at the Sandoz chemical plant in Basel, Switzerland, in 1986, a large quantity of toxic substances leaked into the Rhine. Millions of fish died as a result, and the supply of drinking water from parts of the river had to be stopped.

PCB's and Other Pollutants

In many parts of the world, polluted rivers carry dangerous substances and deposit them in seas and oceans. Many of these substances, including heavy metals such as mercury and cadmium, pesticides, and PCBs, sink down to the mud on the seabed. Microorganisms such as water-fleas and shrimps that feed near the seabed take in these poisons. They are then eaten by small fish that are, in turn, eaten by larger fish. In this way, the poisonous substances are passed up the food chain.

This can also be dangerous to humans, because poisons such as PCBs are not broken down in the bodies of fish. When the fish are caught and eaten by humans, the poisons are again passed along the food chain. In some countries, including Japan and Taiwan, people have been poisoned by PCBs. Many countries have now laid down rules governing the use of PCBs, but these are not always followed. In several developing countries and in Eastern Europe, very high PCB concentrations have been found in the drinking water.

Obtaining clean drinking water in the developing world is a big problem. Many developing nations are in parts of the world where drought is a serious threat. Furthermore, the water that is available is often polluted by untreated sewage that has been pumped directly into rivers and lakes. Bacteria in the polluted water can cause dangerous diseases in people, including cholera. The careless use of fertilizers and pesticides is also responsible for the pollution of drinking water. The World Health Organization (WHO) attempts to help people in many developing countries dig wells for

drinking water. Increasingly, they are finding that the water underground is polluted by agricultural chemicals.

Radioactive pollution

The use of nuclear energy, particularly for generating electricity, has resulted in radioactive waste being allowed to enter the seas and oceans. Radiation has been found to be highly dangerous and can cause serious diseases, including cancers.

Many tests on nuclear weapons have been carried out in the Pacific Ocean. In Micronesia, an area with more than 1,000 islands, over 50 nuclear tests have been carried out since the 1950s. Many islands have been found to be contaminated with radioactivity, and scientists have discovered that many plants and animals have been affected. Many of the islanders are also suffering from illnesses caused by exposure to radioactivity. Some children have been born with deformities or have died within a few days of birth. France is still carrying out nuclear test explosions on the island of Mururoa. The environmental group Greenpeace has campaigned strongly against the tests, but with little success.

Another problem is the dumping of radioactive waste material into the oceans. Radioactive waste is sealed inside concrete containers that are then dumped from ships into the oceans. No one knows for sure how long the containers will remain sealed. If one leaks, radioactivity could contaminate seawater, with extremely serious consequences. A large number of countries have now agreed not to dump nuclear waste into the oceans. Today it is often stored on land,

Left *Villagers in southern India collect their water from the only source of supply, the village pipe.*

Right *A chemical plant pumps polluted water into the sea on the coast of Humberside, England. In the past, many industries regarded seas and rivers as free dumping grounds for waste.*

in old mine workings or in specially constructed storage facilities.

The leakage of radioactive waste water from nuclear power stations and processing plants is also a threat. Faults have occurred at the plant in Sellafield, England, where used nuclear fuel is reprocessed so that some of it can be reused. As a result, an area of 1,160 square miles in the Irish Sea has been polluted with radioactivity. Some scientists believe that children whose fathers work at Sellafield are more likely than other children to suffer from leukemia, a type of cancer.

Greenpeace in action

Greenpeace was founded in 1970 in Vancouver, Canada. Its first actions, in 1972 and 1973, were directed against the nuclear tests carried out by the U.S. underground on the island of Amchitka, in the North Pacific Ocean. They made headlines around the world. Since then, Greenpeace has grown from a small group of volunteers to an international environmental organization with representatives in many countries, including Canada, the U.S., France, the Netherlands, Germany, Britain, Denmark, Australia, and New Zealand.

With its ship, *Sirius,* Greenpeace regularly tries to stop the dumping of chemical and radioactive wastes. The group also campaigns to protect sea mammals, including whales. A number of whale species are threatened with extinction as a result of overfishing, and Greenpeace is fighting to have commercial whaling banned throughout the world.

In 1990 Greenpeace took action against the use of drift nets. These are fishing nets that have a very fine mesh. Widely used by some Asian countries, such as Japan, Taiwan, and the Philippines, drift nets can be up to 30 miles long. They are suspended in the water, forming "walls of death" that trap all but the very smallest sea creatures. They are usually designed to catch tuna fish, but many other fish, seals, and dolphins also become entangled in them. Greenpeace estimates that as many as 100,000 dolphins are killed each year when they are caught in drift nets.

In many parts of the world, the oceans' fish stocks are being reduced by pollution and by overfishing — catching fish when they are still very young and before they have been able to breed. Some fishing grounds have almost been emptied of fish. People are now beginning to realize how much damage is being done. But even if immediate steps are taken to solve the problems, it will be a long time before the ecological balance is restored.

Coastal pollution

The coastal seas around densely populated industrial areas are especially at risk from pollution. In the waters off New York and Tokyo, and in the Irish Sea, countless fish are killed by pollution caused by industrial and domestic wastes dumped in the sea. In these and other areas, fish and shellfish can become so contaminated that they cannot safely be eaten by humans. Mussels caught off New York, Rio de Janeiro, and Minamata (in Japan), for example, have been found to contain dangerous levels of heavy metals. Mercury — one of the most lethal heavy metals — poisoned more than 2,200 people in Minamata in the 1970s. The mercury

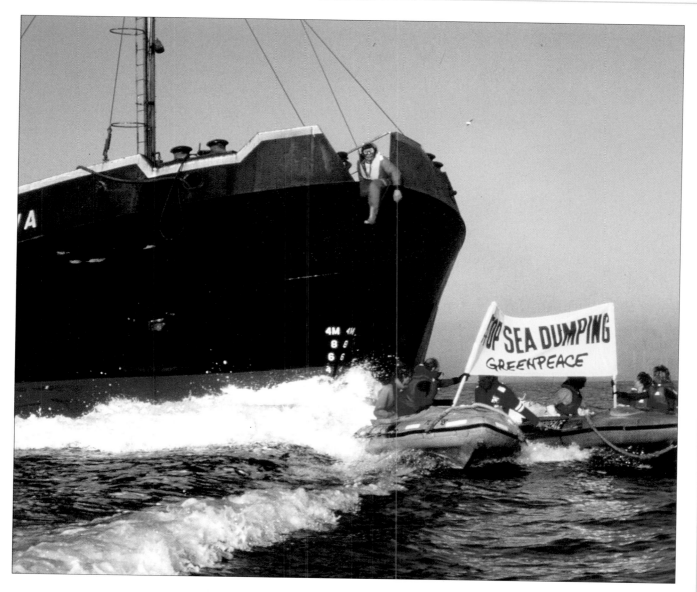

Above *Members of the environmental group Greenpeace protest waste dumping at sea.*

Left *Overfishing and sea pollution have seriously reduced the stocks of many species of fish.*

had accumulated in their bodies because they had eaten fish and shellfish that were contaminated by pollution from a chemical plant.

The Baltic Sea, between Scandinavia, the Baltic countries, and Germany, is the largest area of brackish water in the world. Brackish water is a mixture of salt and fresh, and so saltwater and freshwater creatures live side by side. More than 150 million people live around the Baltic, and they dump vast amounts of pollution into the sea from their homes and industries. As a result, the Baltic has become seriously polluted, especially by untreated sewage, agricultural chemi-

cals, and oil. Baltic fisherman frequently haul up in their nets drums of poison gas, and ammunition that contains lead, dating from the World War II. Many of the drums have corroded, allowing the dangerous gas to enter the seawater. This has had a devastating effect on the environment. Some fish caught in the Baltic are deformed, with a misshapen backbone, two heads or tails, or swellings on their bodies. In 1974 the Helsinki Convention, made up of countries surrounding the Baltic, agreed to reduce the amount of pollution they allowed to flow into the sea.

The North Sea, between Britain and continental Europe, is home to many marine plants and animals. It is the source of 3 million tons of fish each year. Rivers flowing into the North Sea carry a great deal of pollution. The countries around the North Sea have drawn up many environmental treaties and regulations to reduce pollution, but these have not been successful so far.

Left *This bird has been coated in oil following the* Exxon Valdez *disaster in 1989, when an oil super-tanker ran aground on the coast of Alaska.*

Below *As a huge slick spreads out from the* Exxon Valdez, *another vessel attempts to pump some of the remaining oil from the damaged ship.*

In the North Sea there are about 350 oil-drilling platforms. Accidents occur regularly, allowing thousands of barrels of oil to escape into the sea. Many ships carry cargoes of toxic chemicals across the North Sea, and there have been shipping accidents in which these poisonous substances have leaked into the water. Some merchant ships flush out their oil tanks into the sea. Although special aircraft are used to detect such deliberate oil spills, their task is a difficult one, especially at night. Many ports now have depots to collect waste oil from ships. Hopefully, less waste oil will find its way into the sea.

The Mediterranean is an inland sea between Europe and Africa. The water is often seriously polluted because many areas around the Mediterranean pump their sewage directly into it. This is a problem particularly in major tourist areas, such as Spain and Italy, and many beaches are heavily polluted. Vacationers can find themselves swimming in water with a high concentration of sewage, which can cause stomach infections and more serious problems.

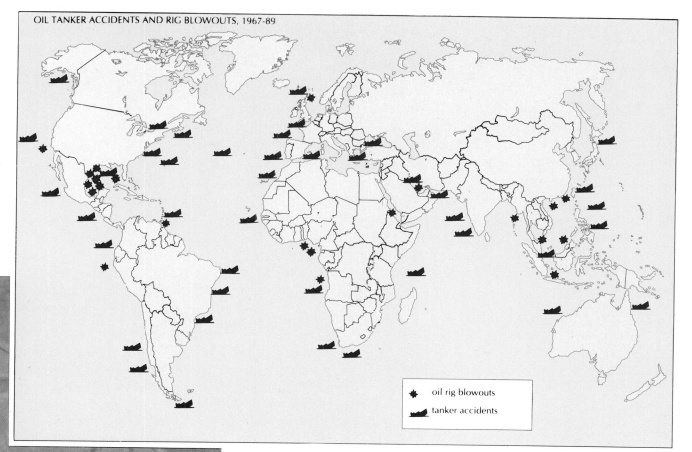

OIL TANKER ACCIDENTS AND RIG BLOWOUTS, 1967-89

* oil rig blowouts

🛢 tanker accidents

Industrial pollution is a major problem for the Mediterranean. Many industrial plants release chemicals into the Mediterranean. In some areas 80 percent of the fish caught suffer from cancer and other diseases. This is a result of contamination by phosphates, PCBs, heavy metals, such as mercury and lead, and pesticides.

Oil disasters

Oil spills from tankers, drilling platforms, and pipelines can cause huge environmental disasters, polluting coasts and killing vast numbers of seabirds and other animals. Along the Dutch North Sea coast alone, more than 40,000 birds die each year from oil pollution.

In March 1989 the supertanker *Exxon Valdez* ran aground in the Prince William Sound, Alaska, spilling almost 12 million gallons of crude oil. Because of bad

Above *The Exxon Valdez disaster was the largest of many tanker accidents. Oil rig blowouts add yet more oil pollution to the oceans.*

weather and the low temperature of the water, it was almost impossible to clean up the oil, and over 1,000 miles of shoreline were heavily polluted. The damage to the environment was made much worse by the slow clean-up operation, and the fishing communities around Prince William Sound suffered an enormous blow.

During the Gulf War in 1991, one of the world's largest oil pollution disasters occurred in the Persian Gulf. Clean-up operations were more difficult even than in the *Exxon Valdez* spill because the slick was in a war zone. Those who worked with wildlife on the shore were on their guard for hidden land mines.

Coral reefs

Coral reefs are unique underwater ecosystems. They occur in warm, shallow tropical seas and consist of tiny living creatures packed together side by side. When coral creatures die, new ones grow on top of them, and so the reef gradually becomes larger.

The Great Barrier Reef, off the east coast of Australia, is the largest coral reef in the world. It extends over 1,200 miles and is home to hundreds of thousands of plants and animals, from microscopic plankton to small fish and large sharks, each of which has its place in the ecosystem. All of these plants and animals can thrive only so long as the balance of the ecosystem is maintained. If the balance is disrupted — by pollution, for example — irreparable damage can be done.

Reefs in many parts of the world are now threatened by pollution, oil-drilling operations, the development of tourist resorts, and by divers collecting shells and corals. In order to protect these stunningly beautiful areas, environmental organizations are hoping to have them designated as underwater nature reserves, like those that already exist on land.

Phosphates

In recent years, phosphates have been widely used in detergents and fabric softeners. When they are flushed down the drain with the used water, phosphates — even those in treated sewage — can find their way into rivers and streams. In these environments they may cause a huge increase in the growth of algae. The algae uses up all the oxygen in the water, and many fish die. Phosphates reaching the sea can cause large "blooms" of algae to develop in the water, killing marine plants and animals, and irritating the skin of swimmers.

Left *Coral reefs are home to countless living creatures. They form very delicate ecosystems that are easily destroyed by pollution and other human activities.*

Below *This river is so heavily polluted that nothing can live in it except the algae that covers the surface.*

More and more detergents are now being manufactured with little or no phosphate — an important step in the right direction. But this solves only a small part of the problem. Phosphates are also found in much greater quantities in other products, especially fertilizers.

In some countries, so much agricultural fertilizer is spread on the land that significant quantities find their way into rivers and the rocks below the surface. As a result, drinking water supplies can become contaminated, putting people's health at risk.

The Netherlands alone produces about 95 million tons of fertilizer each year. Because of the damage caused to the environment, the Dutch authorities have drawn up strict rules governing its use. Fertilizer remains a problem in many parts of the world; as yet very few other countries have begun to tackle it.

CLIMATE UNDER THREAT

As we have seen, the earth is surrounded by a thin layer of gases, water vapor, and dust called the atmosphere. This layer acts like the glass in a greenhouse, allowing sunlight in but preventing heat from escaping quickly. Without the earth's atmosphere the average temperature of the planet would be about -4°F, which is too cold for most living things to survive.

However, what seems to be happening now is that the earth is becoming too hot. It is believed that certain gases that the modern world releases into the atmosphere are trapping too much of the earth's heat. These gases are known as greenhouse gases. The warming of the earth, which most scientists now believe is occurring, is known as global warming.

Global warming will have a major effect on where we live, what food we eat, and how we work. Scientists are warning that over the next century we could experience changes in wind and rainfall patterns, crop yields, growing seasons, the level of water in oceans and lakes, and the distribution of plants and animals.

The world needs to plan for different weather conditions in the next century and cut down on the emission of greenhouse gases immediately.

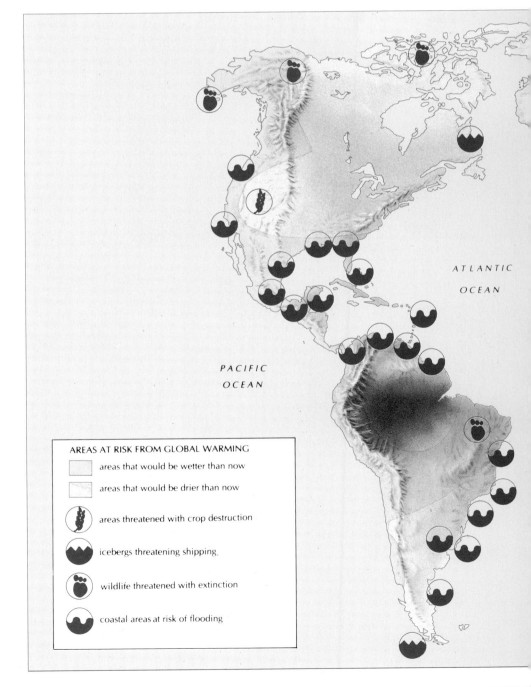

As a result of global warming, the climate in some areas will become drier while other regions will become wetter. This map is shaded to show the projected effect on regions if the amount of carbon dioxide in the atmosphere were twice its present level. The symbols show where the effects of these climatic changes would occur.

If the earth's atmosphere were to heat up by even a few degrees, the Antarctic ice cap would begin to melt and the sea level would rise. Many low-lying coastal areas would vanish beneath the sea.

ATLANTIC OCEAN

PACIFIC OCEAN

AREAS AT RISK FROM GLOBAL WARMING

areas that would be wetter than now

areas that would be drier than now

areas threatened with crop destruction

icebergs threatening shipping.

wildlife threatened with extinction

coastal areas at risk of flooding

How the earth is warming

Since the Industrial Revolution of the eighteenth and nineteenth centuries, many nations have built pollution-producing factories and cut down forests to make way for farmland and cities. The result is that there is now 25 percent more carbon dioxide, methane, and nitrogen oxide in the atmosphere. Unlike naturally occurring oxygen and nitrogen, these gases absorb infrared radiation from the sun, leading to more heat in the atmosphere. As the temperature rises, the warmer air is able to store more moisture in the form of water vapor, which

Left *Freak storms occasionally cause severe flooding in low-lying coastal areas.*

MAIN GREENHOUSE GASES

further increases global warming by keeping in even more heat.

Although the average temperature has risen and fallen during this century, scientists have calculated that it has risen about 1°F since 1900. During the 1980s there were six years of record temperatures, followed by 1990, the warmest year ever recorded.

Sophisticated computers are now being used to try and predict how temperatures might change in the future. In 1990 the world's top experts reported to the United Nations Environment Program that they estimate the average global temperature will rise 2.5°F by 2030 and 5.5°F by 2070. The increase will be greatest closer to the poles because greenhouse gases are more concentrated there. Eventually these higher temperatures will affect the ecological balance of the earth.

Below *Indian villagers protect themselves from the monsoon rain.*

Climatic conditions

All the weather we experience is the result of air movement. As the sun's rays heat the earth, the air above it is warmed. This warm air rises, creating an area of lower pressure below, which is in turn filled by cooler air. This continuous movement of air creates the winds. As the warm air rises it collects moisture from plants and bodies of water such as rivers, lakes, and seas. The air cools as it rises and is able to hold less moisture. The excess moisture falls as rain, snow, or another type of precipitation.

Violent winds and rain can occur in the form of tropical cyclones — also known as hurricanes or typhoons — which occur between 5° and 20° north and south of the equator, where the sea temperature is warm

Above *A satellite picture of Hurricane Gilbert, which began in the Caribbean in September 1988.*

Left *A farmer in the Midwest surveys his withered crops. This area has suffered several periods of severe drought in recent years.*

and the earth's spin creates strong currents in the air. Pushed along by trade winds, hurricanes generally travel westward and often strike population centers such as the Caribbean and the southern U.S., India, and Southeast Asia. As the temperature of the sea rises due to global warming, hurricanes may occur farther from the equator, but so far scientists do not know this for certain. It will take more research and gathering of data before such a conclusion could accurately be drawn.

The changing climate
The weather we experience can be altered by natural climatic changes, events in outerspace, and by human activities. In the Indian region of Rajasthan rainfall has become unreliable, and many scientists believe this is a direct result of the felling of vast areas of forests by farmers. The dry air currents that rise above the ground can no longer pick up additional moisture from the trees and so less rain falls in the region. In contrast, vegetated areas help warm, moist air to rise enabling greater rainfall to reach food crops farther inland.

Some scientists believe weather can be affected hundreds of miles from a deforested region. They have shown that rainfall in tropical forests helps to release natural gases into the upper atmosphere. These elements are thought to help make rainfall occur in other parts of the planet. One computer prediction states that destroying the Amazon rain forest would reduce rainfall by 20 percent and contribute several degrees to global warming.

It seems certain that global warming will change the climatic conditions of the earth, but no one is sure precisely what the changes will be. Undoubtedly warmer air will cause the Antarctic ice cap to begin melting and the level of the oceans will rise, causing some coastal areas to become flooded. It may be that rainfall in temperate zones will increase by 5 to 10 percent, but this is difficult to predict accurately because of other factors. For example, short-term variations in the earth's orbit and the brightness of the sun can change rainfall patterns and the violence of storms. Slight shifts in the earth's tilt, called nutation, can change seasonal temperatures. In the 1990s faster computers and increasing knowledge gained through research will help scientists to develop a more precise picture of climate changes that will occur due to global warming.

Damage to the atmosphere

Human-made elements released into the atmosphere can lead to a series of problems that threaten the climate, as in the case of global warming. However, substances such as chlorofluorocarbons (CFCs) have another, more devastating and immediate effect — the reduction of a form of oxygen, called ozone, in the atmosphere. Ozone is one of the gases in the atmosphere that protects the earth from the harmful radiation produced by the sun. Without this protective filter, ultraviolet, gamma, and cosmic radiation would disrupt the healthy forma-

tion of plant and animal cells on earth. We see the effects of receiving too much ultraviolet radiation when we stay in strong sunlight for too long — we get sunburned. Now there is an increasing awareness that this weaker ozone shield could result in a much higher rate of skin cancer.

Ozone breaks down easily when it reacts with certain other chemicals, such as CFCs. These chemicals have been in common use for many years — as propellants to push ingredients out of aerosol cans, as coolants in refrigerators and air conditioners, and in the manufacture of expanded polystyrene foam. Only 20 years ago, CFCs were regarded as

Below *A three-foot rise in sea level would flood much of Bangladesh.*

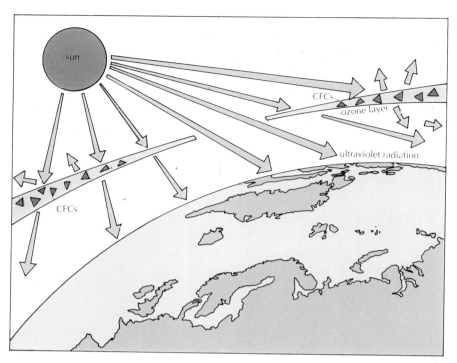

Left *CFCs are broken apart by the sun's rays, producing chlorine atoms. These atoms react with ozone and make still more chlorine. As this continues, more and more ozone is destroyed.*

Below *The Concorde in flight. This supersonic plane contributes in a small way to ozone depletion by adding to the amount of chlorine in the atmosphere.*

wonder substances that were nonflammable, nontoxic, easy to store, and chemically stable.

This view changed in the 1970s when American, Canadian, and British scientists realized that CFCs pose a major threat precisely because they are so stable. As they do not break down, CFCs float unchanged in the atmosphere, rising steadily for about eight years until they reach the ozone layer. Finally they are broken apart by massive amounts of ultraviolet radiation. As they break down, the CFCs release millions of chlorine atoms, which cause chemical reactions that pull apart the molecules of ozone. The chlorine atoms do not change after each reaction, and one atom can destroy 100,000 ozone molecules. The result is a steady depletion of the protective layer of ozone.

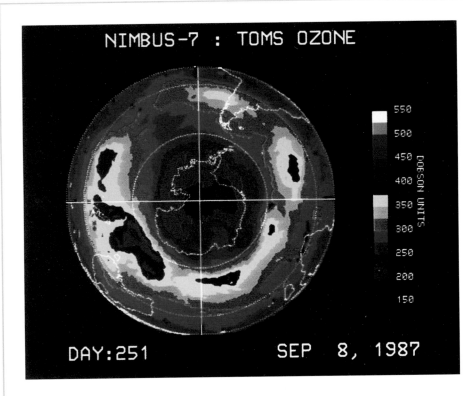

NIMBUS-7 : TOMS OZONE

550
500
450
400
350
300
250
200
150

DOBSON UNITS

DAY:251   SEP 8, 1987

A satellite picture taken in 1987 of the "hole" in the ozone layer above the Antarctic. As more CFCs drift upward through the atmosphere, more ozone will be destroyed.

Holes in the ozone layer

In 1982 a British team working at Halley Bay in the Antarctic discovered that atmospheric ozone was severely reduced in the area. This became known as the "Antarctic Hole." In truth it is not yet a real hole but a large "slice" out of the protective layer, particularly noticeable at lower altitudes. Later studies found that this "hole" is as deep as Mt. Everest and as big as the U.S.

Since 1982, scientists have been using satellites, ground sensors, and even modified high-flying spy planes to discover the cause of the "hole." They have found that high concentrations of chlorine atoms, mainly caused by CFCs, are to blame. Because of unique wind patterns and other factors, the ozone layer above Antarctic is particularly sensitive to the build-up of chlorine. However, it has recently been discovered that the ozone layer above North America, Europe, and Asia is also reduced. Parts of South America, New Zealand, and Australia have suffered ozone reductions of up to 20 percent. As a general rule, it seems that a country's risk of ozone depletion increases with its distance from the equator. European nations and the U.S. view this as a very serious threat to health.

Higher levels of ultraviolet radiation hitting earth will increase the risk of skin cancer, which already kills over 100,000 people each year. It will also affect our immune systems, making it more difficult for the body to fight diseases. Increased radiation reaching the eyes will lead to more people suffering from cataracts. An even more serious threat is the possibility that food crops on land and plankton in the sea will be killed. Without these first links in the food chain, the delicate balance of life could be destroyed.

Solving the problem

Global warming, climate change, and ozone depletion affect the whole world, so it is important that any solutions involve all national governments. Often the United Nations acts as a source for international cooperation.

In 1987 an international agreement called the Montreal Protocol was signed by 81 countries, promising to limit the production of CFCs. However, the problem of the destruction of the ozone layer was so serious that three years later the nations met again and agreed to speed up their efforts: by the year 2000 no CFCs should be produced. Other ozone destroyers, including halon, carbon tetrachloride, and methyl chloroform, will also be phased out.

It will take many years for the ozone layer to recover, because the CFCs released in 1984 or 1985 are only now reaching the upper atmosphere. Nonetheless, international action may have been taken in time to avert a catastrophe giving hope for action on other issues in the 1990s. The U.S. will phase out production of CFCs by the end of 1995. Many nations are now prepared to tackle global warming and to produce a world treaty on the climate in the 1990s. Environmentalists hope that United Nations members will give more money to environmental research programs in this decade.

Hope for the future

Human beings can be destructive, but they can also be remarkably inventive. Scientists are developing new technology to generate power from sources that do not contribute to global warming, including solar, wind, water, and geothermal energy. More households and businesses are becoming concerned about energy waste, and reuse and recycling programs are now operating in many parts of the world. Plans for the 1990s include recycling plastics, reducing paper usage, and developing better insulated glass windows. Because people have shown that they are concerned about environmental problems, governments have reacted with plans for a cleaner and healthier world in the next century.

Right *At this plant the CFCs that are used as a coolant in refrigerators can be removed safely, preventing them from entering the atmosphere.*

Below *Although most CFCs have been produced and used in the developed countries, the depletion of the ozone layer will affect countries throughout the world.*

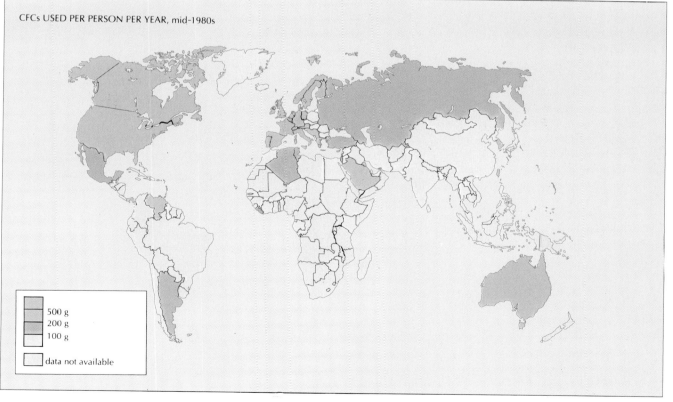

CFCs USED PER PERSON PER YEAR, mid-1980s

500 g
200 g
100 g
data not available

CONSERVING OUR WORLD

Modern technology has given humans the means to exploit the earth's natural resources more than ever before, but, although it has improved the standard of living for some people in the world, the environmental costs have been high. Many wild areas of the world have been destroyed by development such as building, mining, forestry, and agriculture and by pollution of the land, water, and air.
The situation is serious but not hopeless. Many steps are being taken to change and improve the environment. Some of them are international, such as the 1987 Montreal Protocol to limit CFC gases entering the atmosphere; others are national projects, such as the plant-a-tree day in China. Action must be taken by governments and by industries, but much can also be done at a local level — by everyone in his or her everyday life. Environmental problems are caused by ordinary people doing ordinary things. We can all help to solve the problems by changing some of the things we do.

Solar panels

No windows on north-facing wall

Roof insulation

Double-glazed south-facing windows

Heat pump

Heat from soil

Air warmed by sun in south-facing rooms

Saving energy

Using energy wisely is one of the most beneficial actions we can take because energy use is the cornerstone of our lifestyles. We use energy for heating, cooking, and lighting and also for transportation, and running factories and offices.

Being more efficient in the ways energy is used can have an immediate effect on carbon dioxide pollution. For example, between 1973 and 1987, American industries and transportation improved energy efficiency by 26 percent. As a result, carbon emissions stayed at 1.2 million tons a year

Energy usage could be cut by using "passive solar designs" in new homes. This means building them to take maximum advantage of the sun's energy.

rather than increasing. Huge energy savings would result if public transportation and bicycles were used instead of cars, and many countries such as the U.S. and the Netherlands are now improving their mass-transit systems.

In the home, the proper amount of insulation and double-glazing of windows can reduce energy consumption. Many countries

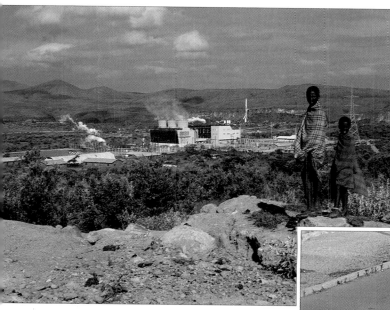

Above *A geothermal power station in Kenya.*

Right *Bottle deposit containers are becoming an increasingly common sight in many countries. The glass is collected and made into new bottles and jars.*

helps to save energy because energy is needed to make all these products.

One effective way of using less is to cut down on waste. A major chemical company, Dow, has set up a "Waste Reduction Always Pays" (WRAP) program. Its aim is to reduce the amount of waste entering the environment and to save the company money. In 1960 Dow created a pound of waste for every pound of product it manufactured. By the 1980s, the company had now have minimum insulation standards for any new home built. Low-energy, long-life light bulbs, energy-efficient washing machines, and fuel-saving vehicles are all now widely available.

Although using less energy is the most important way of saving resources and reducing pollution, the development of renewable energy sources, such as solar, wind, geothermal, and water power, is also vital for the future. Solar collectors are now a source of hot water in several countries, including Israel; the Philippines and New Zealand use geothermal and hydroelectric power as major energy sources; and California has "wind farms" where windmills, or wind turbines, generate over 1,000 megawatts of electricity.

Conserving resources

Using less of everything is another "environmentally conscious" alternative —less water, less food, fewer consumer products such as televisions, cars, and so on. This reduced its waste to one-thousandth of that amount.

It is not only industries that can save resources. Households throw out huge amounts of paper, cans, bottles, plastic, and food. Many of these can be recycled so that the materials can be reused — glass, can, and paper recycling are now common in many towns. Most towns have set up a recycling service that collects glass, cans, and paper from houses every week. Many recycling plants are opening up all over the world. The most technically advanced plant in the U.S. is Rhode Island where 168 tons of newsprint and 210 tons of mixed garbage are processed each day. The plant can recycle some types of plastic bottles as well as aluminum, glass, and tin cans.

Recycling has a promising future — everyone can reduce his or her own waste and take recyclable materials to the local recycling center. It is also important to reuse and repair things rather than throw them away and to buy fewer disposable products. Less

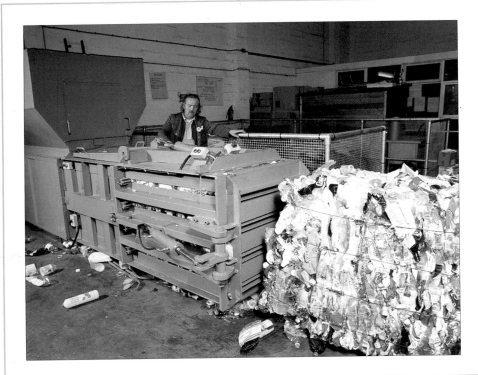

Left *Waste plastics being compressed into bales prior to recycling*

waste costs less money and creates less pollution.

Preventing pollution
Developing cleaner machines and technologies can also make a big difference. In recent years, concern over the "hole" in the ozone layer has led manufacturers to phase out the polluting CFC gases they used as propellants in aerosols and to replace them with other gases or

Right *This map shows just a small number of the species facing extinction; in total, there may be as many as one million. In the past, environmentalists were mainly concerned about the loss of animal species. However, each plant species may support up to 40 animal species, and if the plant becomes extinct so do the animals. As the graph shows, the rate at which species are dying out is increasing dramatically.*

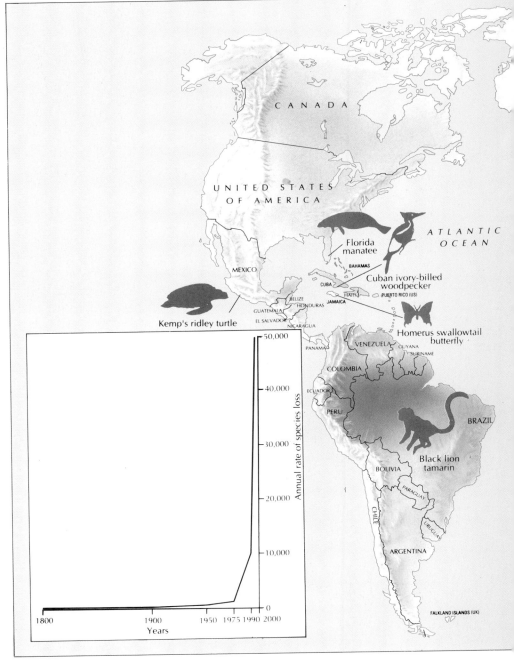

with pump-action containers. Many other industries are following suit and are looking for ways to clean up their production processes. Major industries are spending heavily in order to follow procedures that are safe for the environment.

In stores and supermarkets, more and more "environmentally friendly" household products are being sold. These include biodegradable laundry and dish-washing detergents, organic garden fertilizer, and rechargeable batteries. By choosing carefully what we buy, all of us can help the environment.

For many years, environmental pressure groups such as Friends of the Earth have campaigned to alert people to what is happening to the environment. One campaign urged people not to buy products containing hardwoods from tropical forests and asked them to write to many politicians, decision-makers, and businesses about deforestation. In recent years their hard work has paid off as these issues have become prominent in many countries.

The increase in public concern about the environment has influenced political parties, and many now claim to have environmental policies. Furthermore, many countries have recently introduced protection laws.

Humans and other animals
Since life first began, many animal and plant species have disappeared from the earth. This is called extinction. It is a natural part of evolution and it has happened to millions of species. But the rate of extinction

Barn owl
UK / Denmark /
Germany

Tobias' caddis fly

Chinese
alligator

Baiji dolphin
China

Mountain gorilla
Central Africa

African elephant
Central / E. Africa

Orangutan

Javan rhinoceros

Rock wallaby

Blue whale
S. Atlantic

Tasmanian freshwater
limpet

Eucalyptus
carnabyi

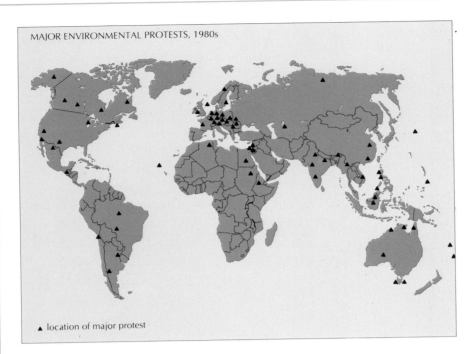

MAJOR ENVIRONMENTAL PROTESTS, 1980s

▲ location of major protest

Left *Throughout the world there have been many major protests about environmental problems such as water and air pollution, acid rain, deforestation, and nuclear power.*

Below *A collection tank for waste oil*

is increasing, and it is a matter of concern that many species become extinct, or are endangered, because of human activity. The most famous example is the dodo. These large, flightless birds once lived on the island of Mauritius, in the Indian Ocean. In the 1600s settlers arrived on the island and hunted the dodos. They also introduced dogs, cats, and rats, which ate the dodos' eggs and chicks. But the 1700s there were no dodos left.

Why conserve wildlife?

Plants and animals on the earth depend on each other to live. Humans are animals, too, although we often forget this, and we also depend on other species for the basics of life such as food, shelter, clothing, medicines, and so on. It is in our own interest to look after other species. Contact with nature is also a source of pleasure and wonder to humans, all types of people, including artists and scientists, have found inspiration in the natural world.

Causes of extinction

The main causes of species becoming extinct or endangered are hunting, loss of habitat, pollution, and destruction by other species that have been introduced either deliberately or accidentally. Hunting was responsible for the near-extinction of the American bison and the Arabian oryx, although both have been saved by captive breeding and reintroduction programs. More recently the plight of rhinos in Africa

has made headlines. They have been hunted ruthlessly for their horns, and the population has been reduced by 70 percent. Animals are often hunted to produce luxury goods, such as reptile skin shoes, fur coats, and ivory carvings.

The destruction of habitats is a major threat to species. Land is taken for agriculture, mining, or forestry, or may be lost because of soil erosion or desertification (the spread of deserts). Development projects can also disrupt the natural territories or migration routes of species. Tropical forests are particularly at risk because they are such rich ecosystems. They are home to more than half of all known species, but they are disappearing at an alarming rate. The creation of protected areas, such as nature reserves and national parks, can help counterbalance this loss of natural habitats.

Pollution can also endanger species. For example, oil spilled from tankers affects marine life such as fish, whales and other marine mammals, and sea birds.

Which species are threatened?

Thousands of animals and plants around the world are threatened with extinction. Usually people hear only about the "famous" threatened species — large mammals such as the giant panda and the African elephant. But most endangered species are little-known insects, reptiles, birds, and plants. There are, for example, over 1,000 threatened mollusk species, and in the plant world estimates are that over 25,000 species are endangered.

Some humans are also threatened. Tribal peoples are often vulnerable. In the sixteenth century there were over 5 million Amerindians living in the Brazil region of South America; today only 250,000 remain and they are constantly under threat from mining and forestry operations.

message is essential, and environmental education programs are run by many organizations worldwide.

Captive breeding programs can save species from extinction. The programs for Goeldi's marmoset, the red-backed squirrel monkey, the brown howler monkey, and the woolly monkey were all successful. Each was bred successfully in captivity. These monkeys will be released into the wild again when the rain forest is safe enough. This method is now being used to help other species whose numbers have been greatly reduced in recent years, including the African black rhino.

Laws are another way of protecting animals and plants. Over 80 countries have signed the Convention on International Trade in Endangered Species (CITES). CITES seeks to stop the trade in threatened species and products made from them. The U.S. has very strict regulations on the import and export of wild animals and plants. Licenses have to be obtained before endangered species can be taken into or out of the country, and then only under special circumstances.

Left *Since 1980 the number of black rhinos in Africa has fallen from 15,000 to under 9,000 because of poaching.*

Below *The Australian rock wallaby is under threat of extinction.*

What is being done?

Accurate information about threatened species is vital, and one organization, the International Union for the Conservation of Nature (World Conservation Union), is monitoring the state of species in the world. It has data on over 30,000 endangered species at its Conservation Monitoring Centre in Cambridge, England, and publishes the Red Data Books, which list those species at risk. Spreading the conservation

Going, Going . . .

• There are between 5 and 8 million different species in the world; only 1.6 million have been identified.
• Over 1,000 large mammals and over 25,000 plants are threatened or endangered. It is estimated that between 40,000 and 60,000 plant species will disappear during the next 50 years.
• Trade is banned in about 675 endangered species and regulated for another 27,000 species.
• The legal trade in wildlife is worth $5 billion per year; the illegal trade is worth $2 billion.

Right *A marine iguana basks in the sun on the Galapagos Islands. Many species on these islands are found nowhere else in the world.*

Unique areas of the world

To protect wildlife and their habitats and to conserve wild and beautiful places, many locations around the world have been declared "protected areas." The first protected area was Yellowstone National Park, which was set up in 1872. Since then many countries have established nature reserves and national parks. Some have been set up to protect the habitat of one important species. For example, the Wulong Reserve in China protects the home of the giant panda. Other areas are established to ensure that a unique landscape, such as the Great Barrier Reef in Australia, is not damaged.

Some protected areas have to be international, because wildlife does not know about national boundaries and frequently cross over them. Reserves often need to be "transboundary," such as the German-Luxembourg Nature Park.

There are also reserves administered by international organizations:

Biosphere reserves are selected because they contain a complete ecosystem rather than any one individual species. The aim is to set up reserves covering all the types of ecosystems in the world. There are over 200 sites listed and many more proposed.

World Heritage Sites are sites that qualify as areas of "outstanding universal value." They are set up by UNESCO under the World Heritage Convention, and countries that sign the convention are allowed to suggest sites. To become a World Heritage Site an area must have either examples of major stages of the earth's evolutionary history, examples of geological processes or biological evolution, rare or outstanding

Below *Some of the world's major protected areas, including World Heritage Sites, Ramsar Sites, biosphere reserves, and national parks.*

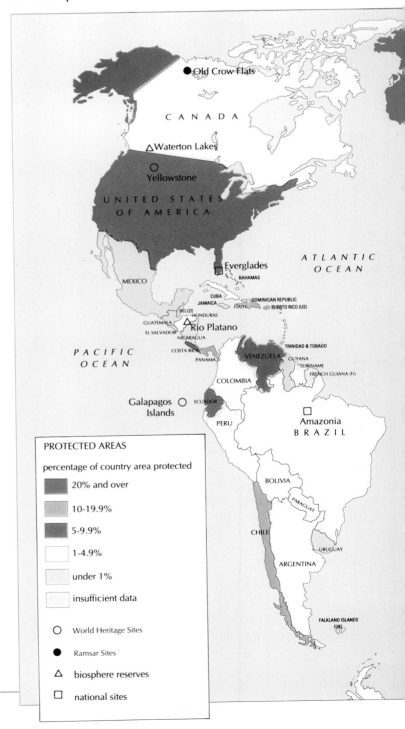

PROTECTED AREAS

percentage of country area protected

- 20% and over
- 10-19.9%
- 5-9.9%
- 1-4.9%
- under 1%
- insufficient data

○ World Heritage Sites
● Ramsar Sites
△ biosphere reserves
□ national sites

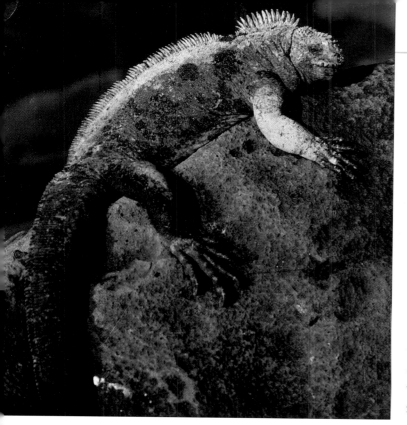

natural scenery, or rare or endangered plant or animal species.

Ramsar Sites. Wetlands, including coastal marshes, river estuaries, and mangrove swamps, are very important habitats, especially for many species of birds. Many birds depend on the wetlands for nesting and rearing their young. The conservation of wetlands was given an international dimension in 1971 when the Convention on Wetlands of International Importance Especially as Waterfowl Habitat was established at Ramsar, Iran. In 1990 the convention had been agreed to by 52 countries. Between them they had listed 445 protected sites covering nearly 75 million acres. This network of protected wetlands is vital to the survival of many plant and animal species.

European Community Special Protection Areas (SPAs) are protected areas for birds in the countries of the European Community (EC). The EC proposes a network of sites in its Directive on the Conservation of Wild Birds and stresses the need to conserve all birds and their habitats.

World Park Antarctica. Antarctica is a unique place in the world. It belongs to no country but is covered by the Antarctic Treaty of 1959, which states that the continent is for "free and non-political scientific research in the interest of all mankind." Many countries now want to start mining operations in Antarctica and do not want the treaty to continue in its present form.

In 1972 a group of conservationists called for Antarctica to be designated a World Park, but this will not become a reality unless the idea is supported by most countries of the world.

Greenpeace has called for Antarctica to be made a World Park, to protect the continent from mining and other human interference.

The environmental group Greenpeace has been campaigning for World Park Antarctica so that this unique wilderness will be protected forever.

Strategies for survival

Making laws is an effective method of protecting the environment. Many countries now have strict laws and regulations on pollution control, wildlife protection, waste management, and energy conservation. There are also international laws, treaties, and conventions to deal with problems such as dumping waste at sea, pollution of the atmosphere, and trade in wildlife.

In 1980 the first global approach to the world's environment was launched by the United Nations, the World Wildlife Fund (now called the World Wide Fund for Nature), and the International Union for the Conservation of Nature (World Conservation Union). This was the World Conservation Strategy (WCS), and it outlined the environmental pressures being put on the Earth, and recommended ways of tackling the massive environmental problems facing

A fin whale is hauled on board a factory ship. Even after worldwide protest the killing of whales continues. Conservationists think there may be only 4,000 fin whales and 1,000 blue whales left.

the planet. Individual countries were encouraged to set up national conservation strategies, and over 30 countries, including Australia, Canada, Nepal, and Costa Rica, have done so. The WCS also called for international cooperation to improve the environment. This document highlighted Antarctica, saying how unique and important it is and calling for "careful study and management of the living resources of Antarctica."

The basis of the WCS was that conservation is linked to development. Development is the term for using the resources of the earth to live, and conservation means caring for the earth to make sure it can still provide the resources that humans need. The difficulty is finding a way to live and improve our standard of living without damaging the environment that supports us. "Our Common Future" is the name of the report by the World Commission on Environment and Development. It was published in 1987 and

again outlined ways to tackle the world's environment and development problems.

The greener future

One thing about which all these reports and strategies agree is the need for a new way of thinking about the world. Many people and countries, especially those in the developed world, have viewed the earth as an unending source of resources for humans to use and as a convenient place in which to dump waste. They have shown little respect for other animals and plants on the planet. This attitude has caused many problems.

The WCS says "a new ethic, embracing plants and animals, as well as people, is required for human societies to live in harmony with the natural world on which they depend for survival and well-being." This may seem a tall order, but it is beginning to happen, as humans slowly become aware of the impact they are having on the earth and the threat to their own survival as a species. It may be that we can rediscover how to live in harmony with nature. In the words of Chief Seattle, nineteenth-century chief of the Suquamish people: "All things are connected. This we know. The earth does not belong to man. Man belongs to the earth."

GLOSSARY

Acid rain All rainfall is slightly acidic, but acid rain is moisture returning to the surface of the earth as rain, snow, or mist that has become more acidic as a result of absorbing pollutants from the air.

Adaptation The process by which organisms change so that they can continue to survive in a changing environment.

Algae A group of tiny, very simple plants that have no roots, stems, or leaves.

Altitude The height of something above sea level.

Arid Dry lands where the annual rainfall is between seven and ten inches.

Atmosphere The thin layer of gases surrounding the earth, mostly made up of nitrogen and oxygen together with small amounts of other gases, water vapor, and dust particles.

Bacteria Tiny single-celled organisms that are very simple in form. Some bacteria cause diseases in plants and animals.

Barren Infertile; land that cannot support crops.

Biodegradable Able to be broken down by the natural processes of decomposition or decay.

Biofuel Fuel from a living source, such as wood, animal manure, and alcohol made from plants.

Biomes Communities of plants and animals that extend over a large area.

Birth rate The number of births per 1,000 people per year.

Cancer A type of disease caused by the growth of abnormal cells in the body of a human or other animal.

Cash crops Crops grown especially to be exported in order to earn money from other countries. They are often grown to pay off debts owed by a poor country to a richer one.

Catalytic converter A small device fitted to the exhaust system of a gas-powered car. It converts toxic substances such as carbon monoxide and hydrocarbons into carbon dioxide and water.

CFCs (chlorofluorocarbons) A group of chemicals that damage the ozone layer. They are used in cooling units, in the manufacture of polystyrene foam, and in some aerosol sprays.

Climate The average weather conditions of a place or region over a long period of time.

Commodities The name given to crops and other goods that are traded on the international market.

Coniferous Trees that bear cones, including pines, firs, spruces, cedars, larches, and cypresses. Most are evergreen.

Conservation The protection and careful use of the resources of the earth so as not to damage the environment.

Contaminate To pollute or make impure.

Continental shelf The ledge of land that juts out around the edges of continents.

Death rate The number of deaths per 1,000 people per year.

Debt crisis A situation, which has built up over the last 20 years, in which developing countries that have borrowed money from developed nations cannot afford to pay the interest on the loans or repay the loans themselves.

Deciduous trees Trees that lose their leaves at the end of the growing season.

Deforestation Clearing large areas of forest without replacing the trees with new ones.

Desertification The process by which land becomes desert, mainly because of overcultivation, overgrazing, or deforestation.

Developed countries Those countries that earn most of their money through industry. They include the U.S., Canada, the countries of Europe, Australia, New Zealand, and Japan. They are also sometimes known as industrialized countries.

Developing countries The poorer countries of the world, which are far less industrialized than the developed countries. Most developing nations are in Africa, Asia, and Latin America.

Dioxins A group of chemicals that include some of the most poisonous chemicals known (consisting of carbon, chlorine, hydrogen, and oxygen).

Domestication The process by which wild plants or animals are brought into use by humans for agricultural purposes.

Ecological balance The stable state in which natural communities of plants and animals exist. The balance is maintained by adaptation of the species, competition between individual organisms and among species, and other interactions between members of the communities and their environment.

Ecology The study of the relationship between living things and their environment.

Ecosystem A community of organisms that interact with each other and the environment in which they live, for example a forest or a pond.

Erosion The wearing away of the land by the rain, rivers, ice, or wind.

Estuary Where a river widens and flows into the sea.

Evergreen Trees that keep their foliage all through the year.

Evolution The slow process of change in the characteristics of organisms from one generation to the next.

Extinction When a species of plant or animal dies out completely.

Fallow A word describing land that is left uncultivated for a period before it is used again.

Famine When people in a region go hungry and may eventually starve because food supplies are scarce.

Fertile A word for soil that is good for growing plants.

Fertilizers Natural or artificial substances added to soil to improve its ability to support crops.

Food chain A chain of living things along which energy is passed as food. A simple example is: grass is eaten by sheep, which are eaten by humans.

Fossil fuels Fuels that were formed millions of years ago by the squeezing of organic (once-living) matter deep underground. Coal, oil, and natural gas are fossil fuels.

Global warming The increase in the earth's temperature caused by the build-up of greenhouse gases in the atmosphere.

Greenhouse effect The process by which the earth's atmosphere allows light from the sun to pass through but prevents heat from escaping into space.

Groundwater Fresh water that is under the ground, contained within the rocks and soil.

Habitat An area, such as a forest or lake, in which plants and animals live.

Hardwood The wood of a broadleaved tree, such as oak, beech, mahogany, or teak.

Heavy metals Certain metals, such as cadmium and mercury, that are poisonous. They are normally stable in the soil but are made unstable by acid rain and can then find their way into the food chain.

Hydroelectricity Electricity generated when flowing water turns a turbine, usually in a dam.

Invertebrates Animals that do not have a backbone.

Irrigation Supplying crop plants with water via channels or pipes in order to help them grow.

Latitude The distance of a place north or south of the equator, measured as an angle from the center of the earth.

Longitude The distance of a place east or west of the prime meridian (0°) — an imaginary line from the North Pole to the South Pole that passes through Greenwich, in London.

Mammals Warm-blooded animals that feed their young on milk produced by the mother.

Migration The movement of people or other animals from one area to another.

Natural selection The process by which the characteristics of an organism that help it to survive and multiply in its environment are passed on to its offspring.

Niche The place of an organism in an ecosystem — where it lives, what it eats, what it is eaten by, and so on.

Nomads People, normally livestock herders, who do not settle in one place but move frequently in search of new grazing or water for their herds.

Nuclear power station A power station in which electricity is made from the decay of radioactive material, such as uranium.

Nutrients Substances, including water and oxygen, that are taken in by a living organism to enable it to grow and repair itself.

Organic farming Farming that does not use artificial fertilizers or pesticides. The soil may be kept fertile by changing regularly the way in which it is used — crop growing, livestock grazing, etc.

Oxygen A gas that makes up 21 percent of the air we breathe. It is essential for life.

Ozone A form of oxygen. At the surface of the earth it is poisonous to plants and animals, but high in the atmosphere it forms a protective layer that keep too much ultraviolet radiation from reaching the earth.

Ozone layer A thin layer of ozone gas in the upper atmosphere that filters out some of the sun's harmful ultraviolet radiation.

Particulates Tiny, often invisible particles of fossil fuel that float in the air when the fuel is not fully burned.

PCBs (polychlorinated biphenyls) A group of highly poisonous chemicals. They are used for cleaning machinery, tanning leather, and for other industrial purposes.

Pesticides Chemicals used for killing plants or animals that attack crops.

pH A measurement of acidity: pH7 is neutral (neither acid nor alkaline), below 7 is acid, and above 7 is alkaline.

Phosphates Chemicals used in fertilizer, some detergents, and other substances.

Photosynthesis The process by which green plants convert water and carbon dioxide into stored chemical energy using the energy of sunlight. Oxygen is given off in the process.

Plankton Tiny plants and animals that drift in the water of lakes, rivers, and the sea. Many fish, and even huge whales, depend on plankton for food.

Pollution The release of materials into the air, water, or land that may upset the ecological balance.

Population The number of things that live in a specific place; for example, the number of people living in a city, an area, a state, a country, or the world.

Radioactive A word to describe a material that gives out dangerous rays, or radiation. when it breaks down or decays.

Rain forest An area of dense tropical forest.

Recycling Processing waste products so that they can be used again.

Renewable energy Sources of energy that do not use up resources that cannot be replaced.

Resource Anything that is useful to living animals and plants.

Savanna A region of tropical grassland, often with scattered trees and bushes. The largest areas of savanna are in Africa and South America.

Sewage A mixture of water and waste materials from homes and industry that is carried in pipes called sewers.

Shanty towns Slum settlements that are built by poor people around the edges of many cities in developing countries.

Softwood The wood of a coniferous tree.

Species A distinct group of plants or animals that are able to breed among themselves but not with members of any other group.

Supertanker A very large, fast tanker ship that can carry more than 75,000 ton of oil.

Sustainable development Economic development and activity that uses the resources available but does not harm them.

Temperate A word describing the mild types of climate found in parts of the world between the tropics and the polar regions.

Terms of trade The level at which prices are fixed for goods that are traded between countries.

Toxic Poisonous.

Tropical A word describing the hot, wet climate in the parts of the world between the tropics, on either side of the equator.

Turbine A machine in which the energy of moving water, steam, or air causes a blade to spin, usually to generate electricity.

Ultraviolet radiation Invisible light from the sun that can damage plants and animals if they are exposed to too much of it.

Urbanization An increase in the proportion of a country's population that lives in towns and cities.

Water cycle The circulation of the earth's water, in which it evaporates from the ocean, lakes, and rivers to the air and turns back to a liquid to fall as rain or snow.

Water table The level of groundwater beneath the earth's surface.

Water vapor Tiny droplets of water suspended in the air.

FURTHER READING

Attenborough, David. *Life on Earth.* Little, Brown, 1979

Bailey, Jill. "Save Our Species" series. Steck-Vaughn, 1991

Baker, Lucy. *Life in the Rainforests.* Watts, 1990

Beckdale, J. *The Climate Crisis — Greenhouse Effect and Ozone Layer,* Franklin Watts, 1989

Bright, Michael. *Vanishing Habitats.* Franklin Watts, 1989

"Conserving Our World" series, Steck-Vaughn, 1991

Crump, Donald J., ed. *The Emerald Realm: Earth's Precious Rain Forests.* National Geographic, 1990

Henricksson, John. *Rachel Carson: The Environmental Movement.* Millbrook, 1991

Javna, John, *Fifty Simple Things Kids Can Do to Save the Earth,* Andrews & McMeel, 1990

Miles, Betty. *Save the Earth: An Action Handbook for Kids.* Knopf, 1991

Tyson, Peter. *Acid Rain.* Chelsea House, 1992

USEFUL ADDRESSES

Canada

Ecology Action Center
1657 Barrington Street
Suite 520, Halifax
Nova Scotia B3J 2A1

Friends of the Earth
251 Laurier Avenue West
Suite 701, Ottawa
Ontario K1P 5J6

Greenpeace
427 Bloor Street West
Toronto, Ontario M5S 1X7

Pollution Probe
12 Madison Avenue
Toronto, Ontario M5R 2S1

World Wide Fund for Nature
60 St. Clair Avenue East, Suite 201
Toronto, Ontario M4T 1N5

International

Greenpeace International
Keizergracht 176
1016 DW Amsterdam
The Netherlands

United Nations Environment Programme (UNEP)
PO Box 30552
Nairobi, Kenya

World Wide Fund for Nature (International),
Information and Education Division,
1196 Gland, Switzerland

United States

Children of the Green Earth
P.O. Box 31550
Seattle, WA 98103

Earth First!
P.O. Box 5871
Tucson, AZ 85703

Earth Island Institute
300 Broadway, Suite 28,
San Francisco, CA 94133-9905

Environmental Defense Fund
257 Park Avenue So.
New York, NY 10010

Friends of the Earth
218 D. Street SE
Washington, D.C. 20003

Greenpeace U.S.A.
1436 U. Street NW
Washington, D.C. 20009

National Audubon Society
950 Third Avenue
New York, NY 10022

National Campaign Against Toxic Hazards
200 P. Street NW
Washington, D.C. 20009

National Wildlife Federation
1400 16th Street, NW
Washington, D.C. 20036

Sierra Club
730 Polk Street
San Francisco, CA 94109

World Environment Center
419 Park Avenue So, Ste. 1404
New York, NY 10016

INDEX

acid rain 30, 54, 58–60, 64, 86
Africa 10, 12, 24, 30, 34, 42, 49, 52, 59, 70
African elephant 87
agriculture 5, 24, 25, 32–39, 50, 82
aid projects 20, 39, 45
Alaska 13, 52, 70, 71
algae 59, 72, 73
angler fish 12, 13
animals 7, 8, 9, 10, 11–12, 13, 22, 23, 27, 28, 58, 59,
    65, 67, 69, 71, 72, 74, 85, 86–89, 91
Antarctica 10, 13, 74, 77, 80, 90
Antarctic Treaty 90
Arctic 11
Asia 30, 35, 42, 49, 51, 80
atmosphere 6, 7, 8, 16, 26, 53, 54, 56, 58, 60, 74–81, 82, 90
Australia 11, 12, 24, 34, 42, 59, 68, 80, 83, 88, 91

bacteria 6, 7, 9, 66
Baltic Sea 69
Bangladesh 30, 78
bicycle 51, 57, 82
biofuel 48, 56
biomes 6, 11
birds 10, 23, 27, 71, 87, 89, 90
Black Forest 31
black rhino 86, 87
Brazil 20, 26, 30, 31, 44, 59, 87
Britain 51, 68, 69, 87
broad-leaved deciduous forests 24
Burkina Faso 17, 44, 47

Canada 24, 27, 28, 42, 51, 58, 59, 68, 91
captive breeding program 87
cash crops 20, 29, 30, 31, 41, 42, 43, 45
cattle grazing 24, 30, 31
Central America 30
chameleons 12
Chernobyl 54
China 15, 33, 49, 51, 52, 59, 63, 82, 88
chlorofluorocarbons (CFCs) 78–79, 80, 82, 84
cities 5, 16–17, 18, 20, 29, 30, 44, 61, 62
climate 5, 6, 10, 11, 26, 27, 51, 74–81
coal 48, 54, 57, 60
Convention on International Trade in Endangered
    Species (CITES) 87
coral reefs 72
Costa Rica 25, 91
crops 17, 25, 30, 32, 34, 36, 41, 43, 74, 80
Czechoslovakia 60

dams 30, 33, 39
debt crisis 20, 44
deforestation 5, 25, 26, 27, 28, 29, 30, 77, 85, 86
Denmark 55, 68
desertification 5, 40–47, 86
deserts 10, 11, 40–47
developed countries 4, 15, 16, 17, 18, 19, 20, 35, 37,
    38, 39, 49, 50, 51, 52, 56, 58, 91
developing countries 5, 16, 17, 18, 20, 35, 38, 49,
    50, 52, 66
development 20, 44, 86, 91
district heating 57
dolphins 37, 68
drift nets 68
drought 36, 42, 45, 47, 66, 76–77
dry tropical forests 24, 30

Egypt 33
endangered species 5, 37, 68, 85–91
energy 5, 9, 21, 48–57, 58, 62, 81, 83, 84
energy conservation 5, 55, 56, 82, 90
energy efficiency 56, 82, 83
environmental protests 86
environmentally friendly products 85
Eskimos 13
Euphrates River 33
Europe 11, 16, 24, 29, 30, 31, 33, 34, 35, 49, 51, 59,
    63, 66, 69, 70, 80
European Community (EC) 30, 58, 87
European Community Special Protection Area (SPAs)
    90
evergreen coniferous forests 24, 27
evolution 8, 85, 89
extinction 5, 8, 37, 68, 84–85, 86, 87
Exxon Valdez 70, 71

famine 17, 32, 43
fertilizers 32, 34, 35, 37, 38–39, 50, 66, 73, 85
fish 10, 37, 60, 66, 68, 69, 71, 72, 87
fishing 36–37
flooding 18, 27, 30, 77
food 16, 17, 20, 23, 25, 28, 29, 32–39, 44, 47, 50, 86
food chain 66, 80
forests 22–31
fossil fuels 48, 51–53, 54, 56, 57, 58, 60, 62
France 37, 67, 68
Friends of the Earth 5, 31, 85
fuelwood 17, 25, 30, 41, 44, 45, 46, 47, 56

Galapagos Islands 89
geothermal power 48, 55, 81, 83
Germany 68, 69
giant panda 87, 88
global warming 26, 56, 57, 74, 75–76, 77–78, 81
governments 18, 29, 30, 31, 61, 63, 80, 80, 81, 82
Grand Canyon 9
Great Barrier Reef 72, 88
Greece 60
greenhouse effect 26, 62
greenhouse gases 26, 74, 76
Greenpeace 67, 68, 69, 90, 91
Green Revolution 38
groundwater 38, 65, 66

habitats, destruction of 5, 32, 86
Hawaiian Islands 10
health care 16, 17, 20
heavy metals 60, 66, 68, 71
Helsinki Convention 69
Himalayas 6, 9, 30
Hungary 63
hurricanes 76–77
hydroelectricity 30, 48, 55, 83

Iceland 55
India 11, 24, 42, 46, 47, 51, 59, 62, 67, 77
Indonesia 21, 30, 51, 59
Industrial Revolution 17, 75
industry 18, 50, 56, 59, 62, 63, 67, 69, 82, 83
insects 6, 7, 9, 23, 27, 60, 87
irrigation 37, 38, 39, 44, 46

Japan 29, 34, 37, 49, 51, 52, 56, 59, 66, 68

Kenya 46
Kilimanjaro, Mt. 11

lakes 30, 53, 59, 60, 64, 65, 74, 76
Latin America 29, 34, 49, 52
lemurs 12
livestock 30, 32, 33, 35, 41, 42, 43, 44, 46
logging 24, 25, 29, 30

Madagascar 12, 28
Malaysia 27, 30, 44, 59
mangrove swamps 24, 89
mechanized farming 17, 32, 37, 50
medicines 25, 28, 86
Mediterranean forests 24
Mediterranean Sea 64, 70, 71
Mexico 20, 42, 43, 63
Micronesia 67
migration 17, 18, 20, 39
minerals 23, 25
mining 24, 30, 54, 82, 86, 87, 90
monsoon forests 24
Montreal Protocol 80, 82
mountains, 9, 12, 27, 40

Namibia 10
national parks 29, 86, 88
natural gas 48, 52, 60, 63
natural selection 8
nature reserves 30, 31, 72, 86
Nepal 34, 91
Netherlands 68, 73, 82
New Zealand 68, 80, 83
Niger 42, 46
Nile River 33
North America 34, 35, 43, 49, 51, 80
North Sea 52, 69–70
nuclear power 48, 54, 66
nuclear waste 54, 66–68

oceans 8, 13, 64, 66, 67–73, 74, 76
oil 20. 48, 51, 53, 56, 57, 63, 69, 86
oil spills 64, 65, 70, 71, 87
overfishing 37, 68, 69
overgrazing 41, 44, 46
Oxfam 47
ozone 5, 53, 61, 78–80
ozone layer 78–80, 84

Pacific Ocean 67, 68
Pakistan 44
Panama Canal 30
PCBs 66, 71
Penans 5, 30
pesticides 32, 35, 37, 38, 39, 50, 66, 71
Philippines 18, 20, 68, 83
phosphates 72–73
photosynthesis 9, 13, 26
plankton 72, 80
plants 7, 8, 9–11, 13, 22, 23, 24, 25, 26, 27, 28, 34, 58,
    59, 61, 65, 67, 69, 72, 76, 85, 86, 87, 88, 89, 91
Poland 37
pollution 5, 18, 32, 37, 38, 52–53, 54, 55, 75, 82, 83, 84,
    86, 87, 90
    air pollution 5, 18, 52–53, 54, 55, 57, 58–63, 75, 82
    radioactive pollution 54, 66–68
    water pollution 5, 18, 37, 38, 64–73, 82, 87
population 14–21, 29, 32, 34, 43
population growth 14, 15, 16, 17, 30, 44, 45
poverty 16, 18, 19, 20, 30, 47, 63

Ramsar Sites 89
recycling 5, 21, 81, 83, 84, 85
renewable energy sources 54–56, 83–84
Rhine River 66
rivers 10, 29, 59, 64, 65, 66, 67, 69, 73, 76
Russia 24, 35, 37, 42, 46, 52, 54

Sahara Desert 40, 47
Sahel 42, 43
savanna 8
Scandinavia 59, 69
Sellafield, England, 68
Senegal 44
Serengeti Plains 8
sewage 64, 66, 69, 70
shanty towns 17
soil 10, 16, 24, 25, 26, 27, 30, 32, 38, 39, 59, 60
soil erosion, 20, 26, 33, 39, 42, 43, 44, 46, 86
solar power 48, 54, 55, 81, 83
solar radiation 58, 75, 76, 78, 79, 80
South America 11, 30, 80
Southeast Asia 10, 24, 28, 29, 77
South Korea 49, 59
Spain 37, 70
sustainable development 21
Switzerland 66

taiga 24
Taiwan 49, 66, 68
temperate rain forest 24
Thailand 28, 30, 57
Three Mile Island 54
tidal power 55
tourism 24, 25, 64, 70, 72
transporation 50–51, 56–57, 60–62, 63, 82, 83
trees 9, 22–31, 42, 46
tropical rain forest 5, 10, 13, 23, 24, 26, 27, 28, 29, 30,
    33–34, 77, 85, 86

United Nations 36, 42, 44, 80, 81, 90
United Nations Environment Program 47, 58, 76
U.S. 9, 24, 34, 42, 44, 46, 51, 54, 55, 58, 60, 61, 77,
    83, 88
U.S.S.R. 49, 51, 52, 54

Venezuela 59

water 6, 10, 13, 16, 20, 26, 65, 67
wave power 55
wetlands 89
whales 37, 68, 87, 91
wilderness areas 13, 88, 90
wind power 48, 55, 81, 83
World Bank 30
World Commission on Environment and Development 91
World Conservation Union 87, 90
World Health Organization 66
World Heritage Sites 88, 89
World Park Antarctica 90
World Wide Fund for Nature 31, 90

Yangtze River 33
Yanomami Indians 13

Zambia 39